DON'T TUG ON SUPERMAN'S CAPE: IN DEFENSE OF CONVENING AUTHORITY SELECTION AND APPOINTMENT OF COURT-MARTIAL PANEL MEMBERS

A Thesis Presented to The Judge Advocate General's School
United States Army in partial satisfaction of the requirements
for the Degree of Master of Laws (LL.M.) in Military Law

The opinions and conclusions expressed herein are those of the author and do not necessarily represent the views of either The Judge Advocate General's School, the United States Army, the Department of Defense, or any other governmental agency.

BY MAJOR CHRISTOPHER W. BEHAN
JUDGE ADVOCATE GENERAL'S CORPS
UNITED STATES ARMY

51ST JUDGE ADVOCATE OFFICER GRADUATE COURSE
APRIL 2003

DON'T TUG ON SUPERMAN'S CAPE:[*] IN DEFENSE OF CONVENING AUTHORITY SELECTION AND APPOINTMENT OF COURT-MARTIAL PANEL MEMBERS

MAJOR CHRISTOPHER W. BEHAN[**]

---

[*] "You don't tug on Superman's cape/You don't spit into the wind/You don't pull the mask off that old Lone Ranger/And you don't mess around with Jim." JIM CROCE, *You Don't Mess Around with Jim, on* YOU DON'T MESS AROUND WITH JIM (ABC Records 1972).

[**] Judge Advocate General's Corps, United States Army. Presently assigned as student, 51st Judge Advocate Officer Graduate School, The Judge Advocate General's School, United States Army, Charlottesville, Virginia. J.D., *magna cum laude*, 1995, Brigham Young University Law School; B.A., *magna cum laude*, 1992, Brigham Young University. Previous assignments include Headquarters, 24th Infantry Division (Mechanized) and Fort Riley, Fort Riley, Kansas (Chief of Administrative and Operational Law, 2001-2002; Chief of Operational Law, 2000-2001; Senior Trial Counsel and Operational Law Attorney, 1999-2000); United States Army Trial Defense Services, Fort Drum Field Office (1998-1999); Headquarters, 10th Mountain Division (Light Infantry) and Fort Drum, Fort Drum, New York (Trial Counsel, 1997-1998; Task Force 2-87 Command Judge Advocate, Sinai, MFO, 1997; Legal Assistance Attorney 1996-1997); 138th Judge Advocate Officer Basic Course, The Judge Advocate General's School, U.S. Army, Charlottesville, Virginia. Member of the bars of Nebraska and the Court of Appeals for the Armed Forces. This article was submitted in partial completion of the Master of Laws requirements of the 51st Judge Advocate Officer Graduate Course. The author gratefully acknowledges the suggestions and assistance of Colonel Lawrence J. Morris and the superb editing skills, support, and patience of Valery Christiansen Behan, Esq.

Table of Contents

An army is a collection of armed men obliged to obey one man. Every enactment, every change of rules which impairs the principle weakens the army, impairs its values, and defeats the very object of its existence.[1]

Yet, when it is proposed that that same general, with those incalculable powers of life and death over his fellow citizens, be permitted to appoint a court for the trial of a soldier who has stolen a watch, oh, no, we can't have that . . .. And I say, if you trust him to command, if you trust him with only the lives and destinies of these millions of citizens under his command, that actually with the future of the country, because if he fails, things are going to be rough, you can certainly trust him with the appointment of a court.[2]

I. Introduction

From the earliest beginnings of our republic, military commanders have played a central role in the administration of military justice. The American military justice system, derived from its British predecessor, predates the Articles of Confederation and the Constitution.[3] Although the system has evolved considerably over the years to its current state of statutory codification in the Uniform Code of Military Justice (UCMJ), one thing has remained constant: courts-martial in the United States military are, and always have been, ad hoc tribunals[4] created and appointed by the order of a commander, called a convening authority,[5]

---

[1] General William Tecumseh Sherman, *quoted in Hearings on H.R. 2498 Before Subcomm. of the House Comm. on Armed Services*, 81st Cong. 789 (1949) (statement of Frederick Bernays Wiener), *reprinted in* INDEX AND LEGISLATIVE HISTORY, UNIFORM CODE OF MILITARY JUSTICE (Hein 2000) [hereinafter *House Hearings*].

[2] *House Hearings, supra* note 1, at 800 (statement of Frederick Bernays Wiener).

[3] *See* WILLIAM WINTHROP, MILITARY LAW AND PRECEDENTS 47 (2d ed. 1920 reprint). Colonel Winthrop notes that the English military tribunal was transplanted to our country prior to the Revolution, recognized and adopted by the Continental Congress, and continued in existence with the Constitution and Congressional implementing legislation of 1789. *Id.*

[4] *See id.* at 49-50 (noting that a court martial is "called into existence by a military order and by a similar order dissolved when its purpose is accomplished . . . transient in its duration and summary in its action").

for the express purpose of considering a set of charges that the commander has referred to the court.[6]

In turn, the members of the court, who in nearly every case are under the command of the convening authority,[7] take an oath to "faithfully and impartially try, according to the evidence, [their] conscience, and the laws applicable to trial by court-martial, the case of the accused" before their court.[8] By their oath, when they sit in judgment in a military courtroom, panel members leave behind the commander who appointed them.[9]

The modern American military justice system is a creature of statutes that draw their authority from Congress's Constitutional responsibility to make "Rules for the Government and Regulation of the land and naval Forces."[10] Its ultimate purpose is to help ensure the

---

[5] MANUAL FOR COURTS-MARTIAL, UNITED STATES, R.C.M. 504(a) (2002) [hereinafter MCM] ("A court-martial is created by a convening order of the convening authority.").

[6] *Id. R.C.M.* 601(a) ("Referral is the order of a convening authority that the charges against an accused will be tried by a specified court-martial.").

[7] *Id. R.C.M.* 503(b)(3).

[8] *Id.* at R.C.M 807(b)(2), Discussion.

[9] It should be noted that to a professional military officer or non-commissioned officer, it is no light thing to take an oath. Herman Melville, no friend of military justice, observed, "But a true military officer is in one particular like a true monk. Not with more of self-abnegation will the latter keep his vows of monastic obedience than the former his vows of allegiance to martial duty." HERMAN MELVILLE, *Billy Budd, Sailor, in* GREAT SHORT WORKS OF HERMAN MELVILLE 481 (1969).

[10] U.S. CONST., art. I, § 8, cl. 14.

security of the nation by means of a well-disciplined military.[11] No other system of justice in our nation carries an equivalent burden.

The modern court-martial has been extensively civilized and, in more ways than not, closely resembles trial in Federal district court.[12] A military judge presides over the court-martial, rules on evidentiary matters and instructs the panel.[13] The court-martial is an adversarial proceeding in which a trial counsel prosecutes the Government's case and the accused is represented either by appointed military defense counsel, a civilian defense counsel, or a combination of the two.[14] The accused in a court-martial, unlike a defendant in the Federal system, has an absolute right to elect trial by judge alone or by a panel.[15] Although there are many functional differences between a court-martial panel and a jury,[16]

---

[11] The Preamble to the Manual for Courts-Martial contains a statement defining the purposes of the military justice system: "The purpose of military law is to promote justice, to assist in maintaining good order and discipline in the armed forces, to promote efficiency and effectiveness in the military establishment, and thereby to strengthen the national security of the United States." MCM, *supra* note 5, pt. I, ¶ 3.

[12] In fact, the UCMJ requires the President of the United States to prescribe rules of procedure and evidence at courts-martial "which shall, so far as he considers practicable, apply the principles of law and the rules of evidence generally recognized in the trial of criminal cases in the United States district courts, but which may not be contrary to or inconsistent with this chapter." UCMJ art. 36(a) (2002).

[13] *See id.* art. 26(a) (listing the requirements for military judges and also some of their duties).

[14] *See id.* art. 38.

[15] *Compare id.* art. 16 (noting that in general and special courts-martial, an accused may be tried either by members or, at his election and with the approval of the military judge, by the military judge alone) *with* FED. R. CRIM. P. 23(a) (requiring approval of the judge and the prosecutor before a defendant is permitted trial by judge alone).

[16] For example, a court-martial panel also performs the judicial function of sentencing the accused. *See* UCMJ art. 51(a) (2002) (setting out the procedure for voting on both findings and sentence); MCM, *supra* note 5, R.C.M. 1005(e)(4) (requiring the military judge to instruct the members that "they are solely responsible for selecting an appropriate sentence"). In addition, the UCMJ still provides for a special court-martial without a military judge, in which a panel of at least three members handles all judicial functions. *See* UCMJ art. 16(2) (2002). Procedurally, the court-martial panel interacts at trial in a manner virtually unknown to the modern American criminal justice system: the panel members are permitted to take notes, question the witnesses, and request witnesses of their own. *See infra* note 579 and accompanying text.

both perform the similar fact-finding role of listening to the evidence and determining guilt or innocence beyond a reasonable doubt.

But there is a fundamental difference that many scholars, observers, and critics of the military justice system find troubling: Pursuant to Article 25(d)(2) of the UCMJ, the convening authority personally selects members of the court who, "in his opinion, are best qualified for the duty by reason of age, education, training, experience, length of service, and judicial temperament."[17] There are no voter-registration or driver's license lists, no venire panels, jury wheels, or random selection of a representative cross-section of the community required in a court-martial under the UCMJ. Members are selected at the will of their commander. The subjective nature of this statutory mandate to select court members according to the personal judgment of the convening authority is, in the words of a former Chief Judge of the United States Court of Appeals for the Armed Forces (CAAF), "the most vulnerable aspect of the court-martial system; the easiest for critics to attack."[18]

And attack they have, on several fronts, in a campaign that began early in the twentieth century,[19] pressed on through the legislative debates surrounding the passage of the UCMJ in 1950,[20] and continues today. The popular press,[21] numerous scholars,[22] and even an

---

[17] UCMJ art. 25(d)(2) (2002).

[18] United States v. Smith, 27 M.J. 242 (C.M.A. 1988) (Cox, J., concurring).

[19] *See infra* note 177 and accompanying text.

[20] *See infra* note 209 and accompanying text.

[21] *See, e.g.*, Edward T. Pound et al., *Unequal Justice*, U.S. NEWS & WORLD REP., Dec. 16, 2002, at 19, 21 (claiming that the convening authority's power to pick jurors is "the Achilles heel" of the system).

independent commission[23] have all waged relentless warfare against convening authority

appointment of court members. The battles have not been confined to our shores. Two of

our closest allies, Canada and Great Britain, whose systems were once very similar to ours,

---

[22] *See, e.g.*, Kevin J. Barry, *A Face Lift (and Much More) for an Aging Beauty: The Cox Commission Recommendation to Rejuvenate the Uniform Code of Military Justice*, 2002 L. REV. M.S.U.-D.C.L. 57 (advocating substantial structural reforms of the military justice system, including removal of the commander from the panel-member selection process); Major Rex R. Brookshire, II, *Juror Selection Under the Uniform Code of Military Justice: Fact and Fiction*, 58 MIL. L. REV. 71 (1972) (advocating a random selection system that fulfills the Article 25 "best-qualified" criteria); Eugene R. Fidell, *A World-Wide Perspective on Change in Military Justice*, 48 A.F. L. REV. 195 (2000) (discussing world-wide changes in various military justice systems and suggesting that the UCMJ fall in with major world trends); Major Guy P. Glazier, *He Called for His Pipe, and He Called for His Bowl, and He Called for His Members Three--Selection of Military Juries by the Sovereign: Impediment to Military Justice*, 157 MIL. L. REV. 1 (1998) (claiming that the statutory panel members selection process is unconstitutional and advocating random panel selection); Kenneth J. Hodson, *Courts-Martial and the Commander*, 10 SAN DIEGO L. REV. 51 (1972-73) (recommending removal of the commander from court-member appointment process and substituting a random selection scheme based on the then-current ABA Standards for Criminal Justice); Major Stephen A. Lamb, *The Court-Martial Panel Selection Process: A Critical Analysis*, 137 MIL. L. REV. 103 (1992) (recommending substantive changes to UCMJ art. 25(d)(2), the establishment of a neutral panel commissioner, and random selection of panel members); Joseph Remcho, *Military Juries: Constitutional Analysis and the Need for Reform*, 47 INDIANA L. J. 143 (1972) (arguing that panel selection system of the UCMJ is in conflict with the Constitution and recommending random selection to solve the problem); David M. Schlueter, *The Twentieth Annual Kenneth J. Hodson Lecture: Military Justice for the 1990s--A Legal System Looking for Respect*, 133 MIL. L. REV. 1 (1991) (observing that the practice of convening authority appointment at least looks bad and noting that a computer-assisted random selection process should not be too difficult to implement); Major Gary C. Smallridge, *The Military Jury Selection Reform Movement*, 1978 THE AIR FORCE L. REV. 343 (discussing the problems inherent with command selection of court-member appointment and recommending changes to panel size and a random selection scheme); Michael I. Spak and Jonathon P. Tomes, *Courts-Martial: Time to Play Taps?*, 28 SW. U. L. REV. 481 (1999) (pessimistically suggesting that nothing can be done to eliminate unlawful command influence and recommending scrapping the UCMJ during peacetime); Colonel James A. Young III, *Revising the Court Member Selection Process*, 163 MIL. L. REV. 91 (2000) (suggesting a random selection system that would eliminate the need for UCMJ art. 25(d)(2) criteria); Matthew J. McCormack, Comment, *Reforming Court-Martial Panel Selection: Why Change Makes Sense for Military Commanders and Military Justice*, 7 GEO. MASON L. REV. 1013 (1999) (arguing that the time has come to remove the convening authority from the panel selection process and substitute random selection). *But see* Brigadier General John S. Cooke, *The Twenty-Sixth Annual Kenneth J. Hodson Lecture: Manual for Courts-Martial 20x*, 156 MIL. L. REV. 1 (1998) (recognizing the perception problem with the court-member selection process but opining that the current system produces better panels than any other system would and asserting that a random selection system could be administratively cumbersome and disruptive of military operations).

[23] *See, e.g.*, HONORABLE WALTER T. COX III ET AL., REPORT OF THE COMMISSION ON THE 50TH ANNIVERSARY OF THE UNIFORM CODE OF MILITARY JUSTICE (May 2001) [hereinafter COX COMMISSION].

have bowed to the judgment of higher courts and removed commanders altogether from the process of convening courts-martial and personally appointing members.[24]

An activist majority of the CAAF recently opened a new front in the war in the controversial case of *United States v. Wiesen*,[25] in which it held that a military judge had abused his discretion in denying a defense challenge for cause of a panel president who had a supervisory relationship over enough of the panel members to form the two-thirds majority necessary to convict.[26] Over the vigorous dissent of Chief Judge Crawford and Senior Judge Sullivan, the majority employed its own implied bias doctrine to significantly limit a commander's ability to select subordinate commanders to serve on panels who might otherwise meet the statutory criteria of age, education, training, experience, length of service, and judicial temperament.[27]

---

[24] *See* R. v. Genereux, 1 S.C.R 259 (1992) (invalidating role of convening authority in Canadian military justice system as a violation of the Canadian Charter of Rights and Freedoms guarantee of an independent and impartial tribunal); Findlay v. United Kingdom, 24 E.H.R.R. 221 (1997) (invalidating role of convening authority in British military justice system as a violation of the European Convention for the Protection of Human Rights and Fundamental Freedoms guarantee of an independent and impartial tribunal).

[25] 56 M.J. 172 (2001), *pet. for recons. denied*, 57 M.J. 48 (2001).

[26] In *Wiesen*, the accused was convicted by a general court-martial of attempted forcible sodomy with a child, indecent acts with a child, and obstruction of justice and was sentenced to twenty years' confinement, a dishonorable discharge, reduction to E-1, and total forfeitures of pay and allowances. The original court-martial panel president was a maneuver brigade commander at Fort Stewart, Georgia. He had either a direct command relationship or potential supervisory relationship over six of the nine court-martial panel members. The military judge conducted a thorough voir dire in which all parties agreed that they would not be influenced by this relationship. The defense counsel challenged the panel president based on the CAAF's implied bias doctrine, and the military judge denied the challenge. The defense counsel used a peremptory challenge to remove the panel president and preserve the issue for appeal. *Wiesen*, 56 M.J. at 173-74. Ironically, the panel that actually heard the case and rendered the verdict and sentence no longer included the original panel president.

[27] *See id.* at 176 ("[I]n this case, the Government has failed to demonstrate that operational deployments or needs precluded other suitable officers from reasonably serving on this panel, thus necessitating the Brigade Commander's participation.") These are factors to be found nowhere in the text of UCMJ Article 25(d)(2) or any of the Rules for Courts-Martial.

Yet Congress has not seen fit to remove from the commander the duty to appoint court-martial members according to subjective criteria. The issue of command appointment of court members existed and was thoroughly debated when Congress created the UCMJ in the late 1940's and early 1950's. From time to time, Congress has re-visited the issue, most recently in 1999 when it directed the Joint Services Committee (JSC) on Military Justice to study random selection of court-martial panel members.[28] The JSC recommended retaining the current system of discretionary command appointment,[29] and Congress has not revisited the issue since.

Moreover, the Article III courts have shown great deference to the collective judgment of Congress matters of military justice. On collateral review, lower Federal courts have found no Constitutional or due process infirmities in the UCMJ's statutory requirement for the convening authority to apply personal judgment, that skill most valued in a commander, to appoint court members.[30]

Thus, even as critics assail the commander's role in selecting panel members, the statute remains intact, undisturbed by either its Congressional keepers or the Article III courts. This paper explores the historical, Constitutional, and practical dimensions of the Congressional decision to maintain command control over the court-member appointment process and

---

[28] Strom Thurmond National Defense Authorization Act for Fiscal Year 1999, Pub. L. No. 105-261, 112 Stat. 1920.

[29] DEPARTMENT OF DEFENSE JOINT SERVICE COMMITTEE ON MILITARY JUSTICE, REPORT ON THE SELECTION OF MEMBERS OF THE ARMED FORCES TO SERVE ON COURTS-MARTIAL (1999) [hereinafter JSC REPORT].

[30] *See, e.g.*, McDonald v. United States, 531 F.2d 490, 493 (Ct. Cl. 1976) (noting that Congress deliberately continued the historical scheme of convening authority panel member appointment over strong objections to the process).

concludes that the system meets the due process standards of an Article I court while permitting Congress to achieve its goal of creating a fair, efficient, and practical system that works worldwide, in garrison or in a deployed environment, in time of peace or at war. Command control of the court-member appointment process is vital to maintaining a system of military justice that balances the needs of the military institution with the rights of the individual.

Section II of this paper will plumb the historical underpinnings and constitutional framework of command control of the court-martial system. Section III will address and defend against contemporary attacks on convening authority panel selection. Section IV will propose a two-phase strategy to help ensure the preservation of convening authority panel selection.

II. Historical and Constitutional Foundations of Court-Martial Panel Selection

The statutory role of the convening authority in appointing court-martial panel members is built on a firm historical foundation that predates the Constitution. Military tradition alone, however, is not sufficient to justify the practice; the Constitution is the only source of power authorizing action by any branch of Government.[31] It is an inescapable historical reality[32] that even as the Framers guaranteed the right of a jury trial both in the text of the

---

[31] Dorr v. United States, 195 U.S. 138, 140 (1904) (noting that the Constitution is the only source of power authorizing action by any branch of Government).

[32] *But see* Glazier, *supra* note 22. Glazier insists that a military panel is actually a jury within the wider definition of the term that he advocates. *Id.* at 17-18. He also asserts that the Supreme Court's long-standing position that neither the Article III nor the 6th Amendment jury trial guarantees apply to the military is wrong. *See generally id.* at 14-31.

Constitution[33] and in the Bill of Rights,[34] they denied it to those serving in the armed forces. And Congress, from the beginning, has retained the long-standing practice of a convening authority personally selecting the members of a court-martial panel.

This section will first review the historical tradition of court-martial panel selection. It will next examine the Constitutional framework for the government of the military. Third, the section will trace the history of Congressional oversight of the panel member selection process. Finally, the section will analyze the statutory due process system of courts-martial in the context of Congressionally created legislative court systems.

A. Historical Development of the American Court-Martial Panel

1. Origins and Nature of Military Tribunals

According to William Winthrop tribunals for the trial of military offenders have "coexisted with the early history of armies."[35] The modern court-martial is deeply rooted in systems that predated written military codes and were designed to bring order and discipline to armed and sometimes barbarous fighting forces.[36]

---

[33] U.S. Const. art. III, § 2, cl. 3.

[34] *Id.* amend. VI.

[35] WINTHROP, *supra* note 3, at 45.

[36] CPT(P) David M. Schlueter, *The Court-Martial: An Historical Survey*, 87 MIL. L. REV. 129 (1980) [hereinafter Schlueter, *The Court-Martial*].

Both the Greeks and the Romans had military justice codes, although no written versions of them remain.[37] Justice in the Roman armies was administered by *magistri militum* or by legionary tribunes, who served either as sole judges or operated with the assistance of councils.[38] Written military codes of various European societies, including Salians, Goths, Lombards, Burgundians, and Bavarians,[39] date back to the fifth century and demonstrate the historical importance of codes and systems of justice in governing armies.

Nearly every form of military tribunal included a trial before a panel or members of some type.[40] During times of peace among the early Germans, the Counts, assisted by assemblages of freemen, conducted judicial proceedings; in time of war, the duty shifted to Dukes or military chiefs, who usually delegated the duty to the priests who accompanied the army.[41] Later, the Germanic system featured regimental courts in which both soldiers and officers were eligible as members. In special cases involving high commanders the King would convene a court consisting of bishops and nobles.[42] The Emperor Frederick III instituted courts-martial proper, *militärgerichts*, in his Articles of 1487, including what Winthrop calls

---

[37] *See* Major Richard D. Rosen, *Civilian Courts and the Military Justice System: Collateral Review of Courts-Martial*, 108 MIL. L. REV. 5, 11 (1985); WINTHROP, *supra* note 3, at 17.

[38] WINTHROP, *supra* note 3, at 45. *See also* Schlueter, *The Court-Martial*, *supra* note 36, at 131.

[39] WINTHROP, *supra* note 3, at 17-18. Winthrop points out that these codes were all civil as well as military, "the civil and military jurisdictions being scarcely distinguished and the civil judges being also military commanders in war." *Id.* at 18.

[40] *See generally id.* at 45-47 (listing several examples of different tribunals and their membership).

[41] *Id.* at 45.

[42] *Id.*

"the remarkable spear court," in which "the assembled regiment passed judgment upon its offenders."[43]

2. Development of British Court-Martial System

a. Court of Chivalry and Code of King Gustavus Adolphus

By far the greatest influence on the modern court-martial, however, came from two different systems, the Court of Chivalry in England and the military code of Sweden's King Gustavus Adolphus.[44] These courts both struck a balance between the demands of good order and discipline and concepts of due process,[45] thereby laying a foundation for modern systems of military justice that strive to do the same.

The Court of Chivalry was derived from the Supreme Court--the *Aula Regis*--that William the Conqueror brought with him to England.[46] The court was physically located with the king and had a broad jurisdictional mandate that included military matters.[47] Under Edward I, the *Aula Regis* was subdivided to provide for a separate military justice forum.[48] This court, known as the Court of Chivalry, featured a panel in which the commander of the

---

[43] *Id.* at 46.

[44] Schlueter, *The Court-Martial, supra* note 36, at 132.

[45] *Id.* at 134.

[46] WINTHROP, *supra* note 3, at 46.

[47] Schlueter, *The Court-Martial, supra* note 36, at 136.

[48] *Id.*

armies served as the lord high constable and presided over a court consisting of the earl marshal, three doctors of civil law, and a clerk-prosecutor.[49] When the constable did not preside over the court, the next-ranking member of the army, the earl marshal, presided over the court; in this guise, the court was considered a military court or court of honor.[50] The court followed the Army into the field during wartime and served as a standing or permanent forum.[51] By the eighteenth century, legislative restrictions caused the Court of Chivalry to fall into disuse; its broad jurisdiction into both civil and criminal matters had infringed too much on the common law courts.[52] It did, however, play a significant role in the development of the British Articles of War.[53]

The Swedish military code of King Gustavus Adolphus, promulgated in 1621, was also tremendously influential in the development of the British Articles,[54] for the simple reason that large numbers of British subjects served as officers and soldiers in the armies of the

---

[49] *Id.* at 136-37. The court had jurisdiction over civil and criminal matters involving both soldiers and camp followers. *See id.*

[50] *Id.* at 137.

[51] *Id.*

[52] *Id.* at 137-38. *See also* WINTHROP, *supra* note 3, at 46.

[53] *See* Schlueter, *The Court-Martial, supra* note 36, at 135 (stating that in its concern for honor and due process, the Court of Chivalry was a significant benchmark in the history of the court-martial).

[54] *See* Edward F. Sherman, *The Civilianization of Military Law*, 22 ME. L. REV. 3 (1970) (noting that the British Articles of War had evolved from the code promulgated by Gustavus Adolphus and not from the English common law).

Swedish king.[55] Many provisions of the British Articles evolved directly from Gustavus Adolphus Code.[56]

The Gustavus Adolphus Code contained explicit provisions concerning the membership of courts-martial, some vestiges of which remain in today's UCMJ.[57] There were two levels of courts-martial, the regimental court (referred to in the Code as the "lower Court")[58] and the standing court-martial (called the "high Court").[59]

The Gustavus Adolphus Code explicitly set out the composition of the regimental court by rank and position. In the cavalry, the commander was president (in his absence, the Captain of the Life-Guards), and the court consisted of "three Captains . . . three Lieutenants, three Cornets, and three Quarter-masters" to form a court-martial panel of thirteen.[60] In the infantry, the court consisted of either the commander or his deputy as president and "two

---

[55] *See* WINTHROP, *supra* note 3, at 19 n.15.

[56] Commenting on the Gustavus Adolphus Code, Winthrop stated:

> In reading these (one hundred and sixty-seven in number), it is readily concluded that not a few of the articles of the English codes of a later date were shaped after this model or suggested by its provisions. In some instances, in our own present articles, there are retained quaint forms of expression identical with terms to be found in this early code as translated.

Id. at 19.

[57] *See, e.g.*, UCMJ art. 16 (2002) (establishing three levels of court-martial: the general court-martial, with a military judge and not less than five members or a military judge alone; the special court-martial, with either three members, a military judge and not less than three members, or a military judge alone; and a summary court-martial, consisting of one commissioned officer).

[58] Code of Articles of King Gustavus Adolphus of Sweden, art. 138, *reprinted in* WINTHROP, *supra* note 3, at 907 [hereinafter Gustavus Adolphus Code]. Note: in directly quoting provisions of the Gustavus Adolphus Code, the original spellings have been preserved.

[59] Schlueter, *The Court-Martial, supra* note 36, at 132-33.

[60] Gustavus Adolphus code, *supra* note 58, art 140.

Captains . . . two Lieutenants, two Ensignes, foure Serjeants, and two Quarter-Masters," again for a panel of thirteen.[61]

The high court likewise had explicit membership requirements. The General served as President of the Court, and members included the "Field-Marshall, . . . the Generall of the Ordinance, . . . Serjeant-Major-Generall . . . Generall of the Horse, . . . Quarter-Master-General . . . and the Muster-Master-Generall" as well as every regimental colonel, men in the Army of good understanding, and even "Colonells of strange Nations."[62]

The two courts differed in jurisdiction. The regimental court handled cases of theft, insubordination, minor offenses, and minor civil issues.[63] The high court handled matters affecting an officer's life or honor,[64] as well as serious offenses, to include treason and conspiracy.[65] If an accused suspected "our lower Court to be partiall anyway,"[66] he could appeal to the high court, which would then decide the matter.[67]

Members of the court-martial were required to take an oath, by which they promised to

---

[61] *Id*. art. 141.

[62] *Id*. art. 143.

[63] Schlueter, *The Court-Martial, supra* note 36, at 134.

[64] *Id*. at 133.

[65] *Id*. at 134.

[66] *Id*. art. 151.

[67] *Id*.

Judge uprightly in all things according to the Lawes of God, or our Nation, and these Articles of Warre, so farre forth as it pleaseth Almight God to give me understanding; neither will I for favour nor for hatred, for good will, feare, ill will, anger, or any gift or bribe whatsoever, judge wrongfully; but judge him free that ought to be free, and doom him guilty that I find guilty.[68]

With very few substantive modifications, this oath carried through the British Articles of War, the American Articles of War, and into the modern UCMJ.

Several aspects of the Gustavus Adolphus Code are significant to the historical development of panel-member selection. First, the Code required direct involvement of the commander both in serving as the president of the court-martial and in selecting the members of the court. Second, the Code established a system that limited the discretion of the commander both in the size and in the composition of the court; for instance, in a regimental court of the infantry, the commander had to select two captains, two lieutenants, two ensigns, four sergeants, and two quartermasters. Third, the Code recognized that in some cases an accused might suspect a regimental court to be biased, and, accordingly, granted the accused a right of appeal to the higher court on that basis.

b. The Mutiny Act and the Articles of War

---

[68] Gustavus Adolphus Code, *supra* note 58, art. 144.

The Court of Chivalry faded into history,[69] but the need for military justice did not. England's rulers still faced "the problem of maintaining military discipline in a widely dispersed army."[70] The solution was to form military courts by issuance of royal commissions or by including special enabling clauses in the commissions of high-ranking commanders.[71] These tribunals eventually became known as courts-martial. These early courts-martial, like those under the Gustavus Adolphus Code, were convened by a commander who also sat on the court as its president.[72] The courts had plenary jurisdiction and operated only in wartime.

The period between the Court of Chivalry and the Mutiny Act was tumultuous, characterized by struggles between the monarchy, which sought to expand the jurisdiction of military tribunals against civilians, and Parliament, which desired to limit significantly the reach of military jurisdiction.[73] In 1642, Parliament promulgated direct legislation authorizing the formation of military courts, appointing a commanding general and 56 other

---

[69] Interestingly, the Court of Chivalry still maintains jurisdiction over questions relating to the right to use armorial ensigns and bearings. It did not sit at all from 1737 to 1954. *See* James Stuart-Smith, *Military Law: Its History, Administration and Practice*, 85 L.Q. REV. 478 (1969), *reprinted in* Bicentennial Issue, MIL. L. REV. 25, 28 (1975).

[70] Schlueter, *The Court-Martial, supra* note 36, at 139. The problems posed by a widely dispersed military remain today. As of September 30, 2002, out of a total strength of 1,411,634 personnel, 230,484 were deployed or stationed overseas. *See* DIRECTORATE FOR INFORMATION OPERATIONS AND REPORTS, DEP'T OF DEFENSE, ACTIVE DUTY MILITARY PERSONNEL STRENGTHS BY REGIONAL AREA AND COUNTRY (Sep. 30, 2002), *available at* http://web1.whs.osd.mil/mmid/m05/hst0902.pdf. Since the information for this report was gathered, the United States has deployed significant forces both to Afghanistan and to Southwest Asia for combat.

[71] Schlueter, *The Court-Martial, supra* note 36, at 139. *Cf.* UCMJ arts. 22-24 (2002) (denominating who may convene general, special, and summary courts-martial).

[72] Schlueter, *The Court-Martial, supra* note 36, at 139.

[73] *Id.* at 138-40.

officers as commissioners to execute military law.[74] Twelve or more of these officers had to

be present to form a quorum, and the tribunal was authorized to appoint a judge advocate,

provost marshal, and other officers considered necessary.[75]

Although it authorized the formation of courts-martial, Parliament never legislatively

created them, fearing that by so doing it would obligate itself to support a standing army.[76]

Charles II, however, was permitted to maintain an army at his own expense. In recognition

of the need to provide discipline for his troops Charles II issued Articles of War.[77] The

Articles of War were not acts of Parliament but were rather issued by the monarch in his

capacity as the executive.[78]

These early Articles of War reflected a concern with due process[79] and panel member

composition. Under the 1686 "English Military Discipline" of James II, for example, a

court-martial had to consist of at least seven officers including the president.[80] There was a

preference for officers in the rank of captain or above; the Code states "[a]nd if it so happen

---

[74] *Id.*

[75] *Id.* at 141.

[76] *Id.* at 141 n.38.

[77] *Id.*

[78] *See id.* at 143. Articles of War had a long history in England. They were generally promulgated directly by the King as an exercise of his royal prerogative, although in some cases the generals commanding the armies of the King were authorized to promulgate their own Articles of War. *See* WINTHROP, *supra* note 3, at 18-19.

[79] Schlueter, *The Court-Martial*, *supra* note 36, at 140 (observing that, over time, the Articles of War evolved and showed "an increased interest in military due process").

[80] Extract from the "English Military Discipline" of James II (1686), *reprinted in* WINTHROP, *supra* note 3, at 919.

that there be not Captains enough to make up that Number, the inferiour Officers may be called in."[81] There was otherwise no limitation on the commander's discretion in appointing the members of the court.

Following the mutiny and desertion of a group of Scottish troops who refused to obey orders to deploy to Holland, Parliament enacted the first Mutiny Act.[82] By the customs of war, the offenses were punishable by death.[83] Domestic law at the time, however, forbade the executive (and the court-martial of the day was solely an instrument of the executive) from adjudging the death penalty in England during time of peace,[84] although courts-martial could adjudge the penalty abroad.[85] Because of the mutiny, Parliament had little trouble enacting a provision that granted courts-martial the ability to adjudge the death penalty for mutiny or desertion domestically, provided that at least nine of thirteen officers present in the tribunal voted for it.[86] The initial Mutiny Act remained in force for seven months, but, with only a relatively minor exception, was renewed annually until it was allowed to expire in 1879.[87]

---

[81] *Id.*

[82] *See* WINTHROP, *supra* note 3, at 19; *see also* Schlueter, *The Court-Martial, supra* note 36, at 142-43.

[83] WINTHROP, *supra* note 3, at 19.

[84] *Id.*

[85] *Id.* at 20.

[86] Schlueter, *The Court-Martial, supra* note 36, at 143; *see also* WINTHROP, *supra* note 3, at 20.

[87] WINTHROP, *supra* note 3, at 20. During its nearly two-hundred year history, there were only two years and ten months, from 1698 to 1701, when the Act was not renewed. *Id.* at 20 n.22.

It became customary to publish the Articles of War, which were promulgated by the executive, alongside the Mutiny Act.[88] In 1712, the Act was extended to Ireland and the colonies.[89] In 1717, Parliament extended the jurisdiction of the court-martial at home.[90] By 1803, Parliament gave a statutory basis to the Articles of War, providing that both the Articles and the Mutiny Act applied at home and abroad.[91]

The Mutiny Act was significant in several respects. First, it provided for courts-martial to adjudge the death penalty at home under certain circumstances.[92] Second, it demonstrated a concern for the composition of the court-martial panel in death penalty cases, requiring the concurrence of at least nine of thirteen officers present. Third, the Act neither superseded the Articles of War nor abrogated the prerogative of the sovereign to create them.[93]

---

[88] *Id.*

[89] Schlueter, *The Court-Martial, supra* note 36, at 143.

[90] *Id.*

[91] *Id; see also* WINTHROP, *supra* note 3, at 20.

[92] *Id.*

[93] *Id.*

c. The 1765 Articles of War: Direct Ancestor of the American System

When war broke out between the American colonists and their British masters, the British were operating under the 1765 version of the Articles of War.[94] This version eventually became the template for military justice in the Continental Army.

The British Articles of War formed a precise code[95] that governed the details of everyday life in the Army[96] and provided a sound method for trying offenses at courts-martial. The Articles of War established two levels of court-martial, the general court-martial[97] and the regimental court-martial.[98]

---

[94] *See* Gordon D. Henderson, *Courts-Martial and the Constitution: The Original Understanding*, 71 HARV. L. REV. 293, 298 n.41 (1957) (noting that the 1765 version of the Articles of War was in force at the outbreak of the Revolutionary War); *see also* British Articles of War of 1765, *reprinted in* WINTHROP, *supra* note 3, at 931 (Winthrop includes a parenthetical explanation that this version of the Articles of War was in place at the outset of the Revolutionary War) [hereinafter 1765 Articles]. *But see* Schlueter, *The Court-Martial*, *supra* note 36, at 145 (stating that a 1774 version of the Articles of War was in place at the outset of the war).

[95] Speaking of the British Articles of War throughout the ages, a distinguished British jurist wrote

> [t]hese statutes are very remarkable. They form an elaborate code, minute in its details to a degree that might serve as a model to anyone drawing up a code of criminal law. . . . anyone who has taken the trouble to look into the Articles of War by which the Army is governed must, I think, do those who framed them the justice to say that they are most elaborate and precise.

Cockburn L.C.J., *quoted in* Stuart-Smith, *supra* note 69, at 27.

[96] *See, e.g.*, 1765 Articles, *supra* note 94, § I, art. I (requiring all officers and soldiers to attend church services); § II, art. V (forbidding officers or soldiers from striking their superiors or disobeying orders, on pain of death or other punishment as directed by a court-martial); § IX, art. III (requiring officers to issue a public proclamation that the inhabitants of towns or villages where troops were quartered should not suffer NCOs or soldiers "to contract Debts beyond what their daily Subsistence will answer" or the debts would not be discharged).

[97] 1765 Articles, *supra* note 94, § XV, arts. I-II.

[98] *Id.* § XV, art. XII.

The general court-martial was convened by "the Commander in Chief or Governor of the Garrison"[99] and consisted of no less than thirteen commissioned officers.[100] In a change from the earlier tribunals under the Code of Gustavus Adolphus and the post-Court of Chivalry courts-martial,[101] the convening authority was no longer permitted to sit on the court as its president.[102] In courts-martial held in Great Britain and Ireland, the president of a general court-martial had to be a field-grade officer.[103] Overseas, if "a Field Officer cannot be had," the next officer in seniority to the commander, but no lower than a captain, could serve as the president.[104]

There were further limitations on panel composition in a general court-martial. A field-grade officer could not be tried by anyone under the rank of captain.[105] Servicemen were entitled to be tried by members of their own branch of service for purely internal disputes or breaches of discipline.[106] Presumably, this provision recognized the principle that officers

---

[99] *Id.* § XV, art. I-II; *cf.* UCMJ, art. 22 (2002) (setting out the requirements for convening a general courts-martial).

[100] *Id.* § XV, arts. I & II; *cf.* UCMJ, art. 16 (2002) (establishing that a general courts-martial with members must consist of a military judge and at least five members).

[101] *See supra* notes 61-64 and accompanying text.

[102] 1765 Articles, *supra* note 94, § XV, arts. I-II (stating that the court-martial president could not be either the commander in chief or governor of the garrison where the offender was tried).

[103] *Id.* § XV, art. I.

[104] *Id.* § XV, art. II. This is a significant provision in its tacit recognition that operational realities could trump the otherwise rigid panel composition requirements of the Articles of War.

[105] *Id.* § XV, art. IX; *cf.* UCMJ, art. 25(d)(1) (2002) ("When it can be avoided, no member of an armed force may be tried by a court-martial any member of which is junior to him in rank or grade.").

[106] 1765 Articles, *supra* note 94, § XV, arts. III and IV. Although this type of provision is no longer a part of American courts-martial practice, it does remain in Army administrative separation procedures for officers and enlisted personnel. *See, e.g.*, U.S. DEP'T OF ARMY, REG. 635-200, ENLISTED PERSONNEL SEPARATIONS para. 2-

belonging to the same branch of service as the offender would have special insight or expertise that would lend a sense of context to the court-martial.

For cases involving disputes between members of the Horse Guards and the Foot Guards, the court-martial would be composed equally of officers belonging to both Corps, the presidency of the court-martial rotating between the Corps by turns.[107] This provision helped ensure, at least nominally, that there was no service-connected bias on the court; an infantryman who struck a cavalryman, for example, would never be tried by a court consisting entirely of either infantrymen (who might be too lenient) or cavalrymen (who might be too harsh).

The regimental court-martial, being a smaller court of more limited jurisdictional concern,[108] had fewer requirements. The regimental court-martial was composed of five officers, "excepting in Cases where that Number [could not] conveniently be assembled," in

---

7b(2) (1 Nov. 2000) (guaranteeing that in separation boards for Reserve Component soldiers, at least one board member will be from a Reserve component); U.S. DEP'T OF ARMY, REG. 600-8-24, OFFICER TRANSFERS AND DISCHARGES para. 4-7 (3 Feb. 2003) (guaranteeing that Reserve Component officers will have at least one Reserve Component board member and also permitting, if reasonably available, special branch officers to have a member of their branch on the board).

[107] 1765 Articles, *supra* note 94, art. IV.

[108] The Regimental court concerned itself with "inflicting corporal Punishments for small Offences." *Id.* § XV, art. XII.

which case three would suffice.[109] The court was convened by the regimental commanding officer, who was prohibited from serving on the court-martial himself.[110]

Other than rank and branch-of-service requirements, there were no other limits on the discretion of the court-martial convening authority in selecting panel members. As for the members themselves, they took an oath, as had their predecessors under the Gustavus Adolphus Code, to render fair and impartial justice:

> I [Name] do swear, that I will duly administer Justice according to the Rules and Articles for the better Government of His Majesty's Forces . . . without Partiality, Favour, or Affection; and if any doubt shall arise, which is not explained by the said Articles or Act of Parliament, according to my Conscience, the best of my Understanding, and the Custom of War in like cases.[111]

The British system of military justice developed considerably over the seven hundred years of its existence.[112] Drawing on civil law sources dating back to the Roman Empire, it created a tradition of military due process in which an accused had the right to receive notice, present a defense, and argue his cause.[113] These rights developed as a system parallel to, and almost entirely outside of, the common law.[114] The court itself evolved from one in which

---

[109] *Id.* § XV, art. XIII.

[110] *Id.*

[111] *Id.* § XV, art. VI.

[112] *See* Schlueter, *supra* note 36, at 144.

[113] *Id.*

[114] *Cf.* Sherman, *supra* note 54, at 3 (noting that the development of courts-martial occurred separately from the development of the common law).

23

the sovereign or convening authority selected the members and served on the court, to one in which the convening authority was barred from court membership and had certain rank and branch of service restrictions placed on him when appointing court members.

Although the British court-martial drew its authority from the sovereign, there had been a struggle between the executive and Parliament with respect to the power of courts-martial over the civilian populace.[115] By first denying capital punishment to the executive, then sanctioning it in a limited fashion through the annual Mutiny Acts, Parliament exerted some civilian control over military justice, giving it "a blessing, of sorts, from the populace,"[116] while ensuring that the span of its jurisdiction was limited. Nevertheless, the Articles of War remained within the prerogative of the executive.

When the United States declared independence and fought the revolutionary war, "it had a ready-made military justice system."[117] It is, perhaps, ironic that even as the fledgling nation fought to free itself from the British political system, it recognized the intrinsic value of the British military justice system in providing good order and discipline to its own armed forces.

---

[115] *See supra* notes 73-74 and accompanying text.

[116] Schlueter, *The Court-Martial, supra* note 36, at 144.

[117] Rosen, *supra* note 37, at 18.

3. Pre-Constitutional American Courts-Martial

The Continental Congress did not wait long before legislatively implementing a code to govern the Continental Army. Significantly, military justice was not left to the executive; in the American system, the legislature undertook the government of the armed forces from the beginning. On 14 June 1775, before it had even appointed a commander-in-chief for the Army, Congress appointed a committee to prepare rules and regulations for the government of the army.[118] The committee reported a set of Articles to Congress on 28 June, and on 30 June, Congress adopted the code.[119] Many of these articles had been copied directly from the Articles of War that had been adopted by the State of Massachusetts for the governance of its troops;[120] in turn, the Massachusetts articles had adapted from the British Articles of War, although the Massachusetts articles were not as complete.[121]

Within a year, George Washington asked his Judge Advocate General to inform Congress that the 1775 Articles were in need of revision because they were insufficient.[122] John Adams drafted the new Articles with the agreement of his fellow committee-member Thomas

---

[118] Henderson, *supra* note 94, at 297.

[119] WINTHROP, *supra* note 3, at 21.

[120] *Id.* at 22.

[121] *See id.* The 1765 British Articles, for example, consisted of twenty sections and a total of 112 Articles. *See generally* 1765 Articles, *supra* note 94. In contrast, the Massachusetts Articles consisted of 52 Articles that were not arranged by sections. *See* The Massachusetts Articles of 1775, *reprinted in* WINTHROP, *supra* note 3, at 947.

[122] 5 JOURNALS OF THE CONTINENTAL CONGRESS, 1774-1789, 670-671, n.2 (Worthington C. Ford et al. eds. 1904-1937) [hereinafter Journals]. The Congress did not indicate in what respect General Washington and his Judge Advocate General considered the 1775 Articles of war insufficient. *See id; see also* Henderson, *supra* note 94, at 298 (citing the Journals).

Jefferson, and Congress adopted them on 20 September 1776.[123] The new set of articles was more complete than the 1775 Articles,[124] closely resembled the British Articles of War, and followed the same format and arrangement as the British articles.[125] John Adams believed that the Articles of War "laid the foundation of a discipline which, in time, brought our troops to a capacity of contending with British veterans, and a rivalry with the best troops of France."[126]

Both the general and regimental courts-martial were copies of their British counterparts. A general court-martial panel consisted of thirteen commissioned officers.[127] The president

---

[123] *See* Journals, *supra* note 122, at 670-71 n.2. Adams wrote that he and Jefferson reported the British Articles in their entirety, and that they were "finally carried" by Congress. *Id. See also* Henderson, *supra* note 94, at 298.

[124] The 1776 Articles consisted of eighteen sections and 101 Articles. *See generally* American Articles of War of 1776, § XIV, art. I., *reprinted in* WINTHROP, *supra* note 3, at 961 [hereinafter 1776 Articles].

[125] WINTHROP, *supra* note 3, at 22. The adoption of the 1776 Articles of War has engendered some controversy. Brigadier General Samuel T. Ansell, in a 1919 article, stated that the American code of military justice was "thoroughly archaic," a "vicious anachronism among our own institutions," that came to us through "a witless adoption" from the British system. Samuel T. Ansell, *Military Justice*, 5 CORNELL L.Q. (1919), *reprinted in* Bicentennial Issue, MIL. L. REV. 53, 67 (1975). In support of those conclusions, Ansell quoted John Adams, who reported the 1776 revisions to Congress:

> There was extant, I observed, one system of Articles of War which had carried two empires to the head of mankind, the Roman and the British: for the British Articles of War are only a literal translation of the Roman. It would be vain for us to seek in our own invention or the records of warlike nations for a more complete system of military discipline. I was, therefore, for reporting the British Articles of War totidem verbis ****. So undigested were the notions of liberty prevalent among the majority of the members most zealously attached to the public cause that to this day I scarcely know how it was possible that these articles should have been carried. They were adopted, however, and they have governed our armies with little variation to this day.

Id. at 55-56, (quoting 3 JOHN ADAMS, HISTORY OF THE ADOPTION OF THE BRITISH ARTICLES OF 1774 BY THE CONTINENTAL CONGRESS: LIFE AND WORKS OF JOHN ADAMS, 68-82).

[126] Journals, *supra* note 122, at 671 n.2. Interestingly, this sentence is part of the material that General Ansell omitted when quoting the same letter in his 1919 Cornell Law Quarterly Article. Perhaps it did not fit his theory of a "witless adoption" of a "vicious anachronism."

[127] 1776 Articles, *supra* note 124, § XIV, art. I.

could not be the convening authority and had to be a field grade officer;[128] however, unlike the 1765 British Articles, there was no "military exigency" exception permitting captains as courts-martial presidents.[129] Field grade officers could not be tried by anyone lower in rank than a captain.[130] When soldiers in a dispute belonged to different corps, the court-martial was required to be composed equally of members of both corps, with a rotating presidency between the corps.[131]

The regimental court-martial was also nearly identical to its British counterpart. It consisted of five officers, unless that number could not conveniently be assembled, in which case three would do.[132] The regimental commander--the convening authority--could not be a member of the court-martial.[133] In addition, the court members took an oath that did not differ appreciably from that in the British Articles of War, promising to "duly administer justice . . . without partiality, favor, or affection" and to use their "conscience, the best of [their] understanding, and the custom of war in like cases."[134]

The 1776 Articles remained in place for ten years before Congress made revisions to reflect the realities of military life in America. In an army that relied on small, independent

---

[128] *Id.*

[129] *See supra* note 104 and accompanying text.

[130] 1776 Articles, *supra* note 124, § XIV, art. 7.

[131] *Id.* § XIV, art. 9

[132] *Id.* § XIV, art. 11.

[133] *Id.*

[134] *Id.* § XIV, art. 3.

detachments, it was not always possible to comply with the strict size requirements for courts-martial mandated by the 1776 Articles.[135] The minimum size of a court-martial panel shrunk dramatically, from thirteen to five.[136] The 1786 Articles provided that no officer could be tried by anything less than a general court-martial.[137] The restriction against field grade officers being tried by anyone of a lower rank than captain disappeared, replaced by the aspirational requirement, "No officer shall be tried by . . . officers of an inferior rank if it can be avoided."[138] Regimental courts-martial panels were reduced to three.[139] In addition, a new category of court, the garrison court, was created, also consisting of a panel of three;[140] the garrison court applied to all "garrisons, forts, barracks, or other place[s]" where the troops came from different corps.[141] The changes to panel size have remained a part of our system to this day.[142]

---

[135] American Articles of 1786, *reprinted in* WINTHROP, *supra* note 3, at 972 [hereinafter 1786 Articles]. In the preamble to the revision, Congress noted that

> [C]rimes may be committed by officers and soldiers serving with small detachments of the forces of the United States, and where there may not be a sufficient number of officers to hold a general court-martial, according to the rules and articles of war, in consequence of which criminals may escape punishment, to the great injury of the discipline of the troops and the public service.

Id. pmbl.

[136] *Id.* art. 1.

[137] *Id.* art. 11.

[138] *Id.*

[139] *Id.* art. 3.

[140] *Id.*

[141] *Id.*

[142] *See* UCMJ art. 16 (2002) (establishing the size of a general courts-martial panel as not less than five members and a special courts-martial panel as not less than three members).

The pre-constitutional American Articles of War drew heavily on the British Articles in both form and substance, but even before the Constitutional Convention, the American system had broken away from its British counterpart in significant ways. First, the American Articles of War, although borrowed almost directly from the British, were a legislative enactment and not an executive order. Second, Congress demonstrated its flexibility and willingness to change the Articles as necessary. When the 1775 articles proved inadequate, Congress acceded to a request from the commanding general of the Continental Army, George Washington, and changed them, resulting in the 1776 articles. Ten years later, Congress evinced a willingness to revise the articles to reflect the reality of a small military that operated from a number of small, isolated detachments and garrisons. Independence having been obtained, the stage was set for the Framers to create a "more perfect Union"[143] and to assign the military its proper place within it.

B. Constitutional Framework for the Government of the Military: An American Innovation

The Founding Fathers were well aware of the power struggle that had existed between Parliament and the King regarding the powers of the military. Likewise, many of them were combat veterans who had served in the Continental Army and understood the demands of military life and the need for a well-disciplined fighting force. Their solution for the government of the armed forces was a classic balancing of Constitutional interests and powers. Through a combination of structural grants of power and legislation, they assured

---

[143] U.S. CONST. pmbl.

29

that Congress--with its responsiveness to the population, its fact-finding ability, and its collective deliberative processes--would provide for the government of the armed forces.

1. The Articles of Confederation and Legislative Government of the Armed Forces

One of the first acts of the Continental Congress was to provide rules and regulations for the Continental Army. On 14 June 1775, Congress appointed a committee to prepare rules and regulations for the government of the Army.[144] On 15 June 1775, Congress unanimously elected George Washington to be Commander-in-Chief of the army.[145] George Washington's commission as commander-in-chief required him to ensure "strict discipline and order to be observed in the army . . . and . . . to regulate [his] conduct, in every respect, by the rules and discipline of war, (as herewith given [him]) . . . ."[146]

In 1777, the Articles of Confederation were drafted. The Articles themselves would prove defective in forming a central government with sufficient authority to bind together a nation.[147] Nevertheless, the Articles formalized the powers that Congress had already exercised with respect to the military. Article IX granted Congress the "exclusive right and

---

[144] *See* Henderson, *supra* note 94, at 298.

[145] *Id.*

[146] 2 JOUR. CONT. CONG. 85, 96 (1775), *quoted in* Henderson, *supra* note 94, at 298.

[147] *See generally* RALPH MITCHELL, CONGRESSIONAL QUARTERLY, CQ'S GUIDE TO THE U.S. CONSTITUTION 5-7 (1986).

power of . . . making rules for the government and regulation of the said land and naval forces, and directing their operations."[148]

Article IX had a substantive impact on history. The Continental Congress was heavily involved in the day-to-day operations of the Revolutionary War and, from time to time, directed that certain members of the Continental Army and Navy be tried by court-martial.[149] Problems with desertion from the regular and militia forces required Congress continually to focus its attention on disciplinary matters.[150] By the end of the war, it could truly be said that the "leaders and participants in the American Revolution were no strangers to the articles of war and the court-martial."[151]

2. The Constitutional Balance for Government of the Armed Forces

One of the great defects of the Articles of Confederation was their failure to provide for the separate functions of the three basic branches of government--executive, legislative, and judicial.[152] The Constitutional Convention of 1787 set out to remedy this problem, creating a government in which the separate branches of power served as a check and balance on each

---

[148] U.S. ARTS. OF CONFED. art. IX, para. 4 (1777), *quoted in* Henderson, *supra* note 94, at 298.

[149] Eugene M. Van Loan III, *The Jury, the Court-Martial, and the Constitution*, 57 CORNELL L. REV. 363, 383 (1971-1972).

[150] *Id.*

[151] *Id.* at 384.

[152] *See* MITCHELL, *supra* note 147, at 14.

other.[153] Principles of separation of powers also applied to the military. In arranging for the command, control, funding, and government of the armed forces, the Framers vested power in the executive and legislative branches but left the judiciary with only a collateral role in governing the armed forces.

The Constitution vested overall command of the armed forces in the President in Article II: "The President shall be Commander in Chief of the Army and Navy of the United States, and of the Militia of the several states, when called into the actual Service of the United States."[154] The President did not, however, have plenary power over the armed forces; significant functions were delegated to the legislative branch.[155] In Article I, Congress was granted the power "To make Rules for the Government and Regulation of the land and naval Forces."[156] This provision was added without debate directly to the Constitution from the existing Articles of Confederation[157] and indicates an unbroken link of legislative control over the government of the armed forces from the beginnings of the republic.

By distributing power over the armed forces between the legislative and executive branches, the Framers nicely "avoided much of the political-military power struggle which

---

[153] *Id.*

[154] U.S. CONST. art. II, § 2, cl. 1.

[155] For example, Congress has the power to raise and support armies, to provide and maintain a Navy, to call forth the militia to suppress insurrections and repel invasions, to provide for the organization and discipline of the militia, and to declare war. *Id.* art. I, § 8.

[156] *Id.* art. I, § 8, cl. 14.

[157] Van Loan III, *supra* note 149, at 384.

typified so much of the early history of the British court-martial system."[158] They made it clear that while overall command of the military rested with the executive, the military would be governed and regulated according to the law handed down by the legislative branch. Thus, government of the armed forces would always reflect the will of the people as expressed through their representatives in Congress.

Following ratification of the Constitution, the First Congress undertook legislative action to provide "rules for the government and regulation of the armed forces." By an enactment of 29 September 1789, the Congress expressly adopted the Articles of War that were already in force to govern the army.[159] Thus, it can fairly be said that

> Congress did not originally create the court-martial, but, by the operation of the Act . . ., continued it in existence as previously established. Thus, as already indicated, this court is perceived to be in fact older than the Constitution, and therefore older than any court of the United States instituted or authorized by that instrument.[160]

The age and history of courts-martial in the United States, as well as the customs and traditions pertaining thereto, are of no small significance in weighing challenges to the practice of command control over the appointment of court-martial members.

Having established the historical roots of the court-martial, its place in pre-Constitutional American history, and its firm basis in the legislative branch of government, we will now

---

[158] Schlueter, *The Court-Martial, supra* note 36, at 149.

[159] WINTHROP, *supra* note 3, at 23.

[160] *See id.* at 47-48.

turn our attention to Congressional oversight of the practice of discretionary command appointment of courts-martial panel members.

C. Congressional Oversight of Panel-Member Selection Process

In over two hundred and twenty-five years of Congressional control over the courts-martial system, the practice of discretionary command appointment of court-martial members--one of the salient features of military justice--has survived every attack. This section will discuss Congressional management of the court-member appointment process from the 1786 Articles of War to the present day. Over the years, Congress has statutorily limited the discretion of the convening authority and created a justice system that seeks to balance the legitimate needs of the military with the demands of due process.

1. 1789 to 1916: A Period of Limited Oversight

Congress revised the Articles of War in 1806, 1874 and 1916, but by and large, the substantive laws and procedural rules of military justice changed very little from the Articles of War passed by the Continental Congress in 1775 and adopted by Congress in 1789.[161]

---

[161] Sherman, *supra* note 54, at 10. Sherman notes that although the Army and Navy justice systems differed at times in terminology, substantive law, and procedure, they each shared the following general characteristics: (1) Each contained a statement of crimes and punishments; (2) Each began with preferral of charges, and by the late 19th century, a nominal pretrial investigation was required; (3) The commander made the determination of whether or not to have a court-martial, appointed the court, oversaw the administration of the trial, and reviewed the decision and sentence; (4) The commander appointed court members from his command, with virtually no limits on his discretion; (5) There was no judge, so the court carried out its own judicial functions; (6) There was no right to defense counsel, although a non-lawyer officer was often appointed as a defense counsel in general courts-martial; (7) The court-martial tended to resemble an administrative proceeding more than a judicial proceeding in a court; and (8) The convening authority was also the final review authority post-trial, except in cases where the sentence involved dismissal of an officer, death, or cases involving generals, in which case the sentence could not be executed without presidential confirmation. *Id.* at 10-14.

Nevertheless, Congress did exercise oversight over the process, making some changes to the system to reflect the needs of the service.

Congress made few substantive changes to courts-martial composition in the 1806 Articles of War. However, the 1806 Articles did contain a provision that officers of the Marine Corps and officers of the Army,[162] "when convenient and necessary to the public service," should be associated with each other for the purposes of trying courts-martial, and "the orders of the senior officer of either corps who may be present and duly authorized, shall be received and obeyed."[163] The 1806 Articles also granted the accused the right to challenge a member of the court, and the court was bound, "after due deliberation, [to] determine the relevancy or validity, and decide accordingly."[164] The right to individually challenge a member of the court had not previously existed.

---

[162] Winthrop explains that prior to legislation enacted in 1834, the Marine Corps had occupied an undefined position. In 1834, the Marine Corps was assimilated to the Army with respect to rank, organization, discipline and pay, but was permanently attached to the Navy for jurisdictional and disciplinary purposes. He cites occasions in which the Marines were detached for service with the Army, including considerable periods during the war in Mexico, and the taking of Fort Fisher during the Civil War. Given the potential for Marines to serve with the Army, it was deemed expedient to permit Marines and Army personnel to serve on courts-martial together. He also relates a case where a Marine lieutenant colonel was court-martialed by the Army, and despite a holding by the Attorney General that he could legally be tried by a court consisting entirely of Army officers, it was deemed prudent to put two Marines on the court-martial. *See* WINTHROP, *supra* note 3, at 74-75.

[163] American Articles of War of 1806, art. 68, *reprinted in* WINTHROP, *supra* note 3, at 976 [hereinafter 1806 Articles]. *Cf. supra* note 107 and accompanying text (discussion of British provision that in disputes between members of the infantry and cavalry, the accused was entitled to equal representation by each on his court-martial panel).

[164] 1806 Articles, *supra* note 163, art. 71.

The 1874 Articles added provisions pertaining to the authority to convene courts-martial[165] and created a new type of court-martial, the field officer court.[166] In time of war, every regiment would detail a field officer as a one-man court to handle offenses by soldiers in the regiment. No regimental or garrison courts-martial could be held when a field officer court could be convened.[167] The 1874 Articles retained the provision permitting Army and Marine Corps officers detached to Army service to serve together on courts-martial,[168] but added a provision that Regular Army officers would not otherwise be competent to sit on courts-martial to try the officers or soldiers of another force.[169]

The 1916 changes were more sweeping. Congress provided general, special, and summary courts-martial, the three forms of courts-martial still in force today.[170] In addition, Congress revised the requirements to convene the different types of courts-martial.[171] As in

---

[165] *See* American Articles of War of 1874, art. 72 (granting general courts-martial convening authority to the commander of an army, Territorial Division, or department) *and* art. 73 (granting general courts-martial convening authority to commanders of divisions and separate brigades), *reprinted in* WINTHROP, *supra* note 3, at 986 [hereinafter 1874 Articles].

[166] *Id.* art. 80.

[167] *Id.*

[168] *Id.* art. 78.

[169] *Id.* art. 77.

[170] American Articles of War of 1916, *in* Army Appropriations Act of 1916, Pub. L. No. 64-242, § 3, 39 Stat. 619, 650-670, art. 3 (1916) [hereinafter 1916 Articles]. General courts-martial were to consist of between five and thirteen officers, special courts of three to five officers, and summary courts of one officer. *See id.* arts. 5-7. Compare today's UCMJ, which classifies the modern courts-martial and establishes their membership as follows: General courts-martial, a military judge alone or at least five members and a military judge; special courts-martial, a military judge alone, military judge with three members, or three members alone; summary court-martial, one summary court officer. *See* UCMJ art. 16 (2002).

[171] General courts-martial could be convened by separate brigade or district commanders and higher commanders, including the President; special courts-martial could be convened by the commander of a detached battalion or other command; and summary courts-martial could be convened by the commander of a

the past, all Army officers and Marines detached for Army service were eligible to serve on courts-martial panels.[172] Otherwise, there were no limitations on the convening authority's discretion in selecting panel members.

2. Post-World-War I Revisions: Introduction of Statutory Selection Criteria

The 1916 Articles "did not wholly stand the testing fires"[173] of World War I. The massive mobilizations of the war brought large numbers of soldiers and officers into the Army who had little experience with military justice. The officers, in particular, were prone as commanders to resort too readily to courts-martial, and as panel members to avoid responsibility by giving severe sentences accompanied with recommendations for clemency.[174] When the troops returned home, they brought with them stories "of tyrannical oppression, arrant miscarriages of justice, and a complete absence of any means whereby the wronged individual could obtain recourse."[175] The public was outraged, and for the first time in U.S. history, there was a public movement to civilianize military law.[176]

---

detached company or other command. *See* 1916 Articles, *supra* note 170, arts. 8-10. Compare with UCMJ arts. 22-24 (2002), which continue virtually the same system of courts-martial convening authorities.

[172] 1916 Articles, *supra* note 170, art. 4.

[173] Schlueter, *The Court-Martial*, *supra* note 36, at 157.

[174] *See* Young, *supra* note 22, at 100.

[175] Arthur E. Farmer & Richard H. Wels, *Command Control--Or Military Justice?* 24 N.Y.U. L.Q. REV. 263, 264 (1949). The real irony of the movement for reform is that many of the abuses were likely committed not by career officers with a sound understanding of military justice and discipline, but by newly anointed civilian officers whose mistaken beliefs about military justice turned them into martinets.

[176] Sherman, *supra* note 54, at 5. The post-World War I experience would set a pattern for the rest of the twentieth century: Great numbers of draftee citizen-soldiers would participate in a conflict, return home

The controversy spawned the famous Ansell-Crowder dispute, in which Major General Enoch Crowder, The Judge Advocate General, weighed in on behalf of the status quo and Brigadier General Samuel T. Ansell, The Acting Judge Advocate General, espoused the view that the military justice system was un-American and needed to be changed.[177] Ansell sought a number of changes, including an independent military judge who would select the court members, the right of the accused to have a portion of the panel chosen from his own rank, definite limits on sentences, mandatory and binding pretrial investigations, right to legal counsel, and a civilian court of appeals.[178]

After demobilization, the movement lost some of its momentum, and what began as an overhaul of the military justice system ended as merely a revision.[179] Congress enacted a new set of Articles of War on 4 June 1920.[180] The new Articles permitted enlisted men to prefer charges,[181] required an impartial investigation prior to referring charges to trial,[182] provided for a law member to serve on courts-martial,[183] guaranteed counsel for the

---

disenchanted with a military justice system that was foreign to their civilian experience, and the public would agitate for change.

[177] *See* Farmer & Wels, *supra* note 175, at 264.

[178] Sherman, *supra* note 54, at 6.

[179] Young, *supra* note 22, at 100.

[180] 1920 Articles of War, *in* Pub. L. No. 66-242, ch. II, 41 Stat. 759, 787-812 (1920) [hereinafter 1920 Articles]. None of these changes affected the Articles for the Government of the Navy. *See* Farmer & Wels, *supra* note 175, at 264.

[181] *See* 1920 Articles, *supra* note 180, art. 70 (providing that "[c]harges and specifications must be signed by a person subject to military law").

[182] *Id.*

[183] *Id.* art. 8. A law member performed duties analogous to those of a modern-day military judge.

accused,[184] established the appointment of a judge advocate to serve as a prosecuting attorney,[185] and set up a system to review courts-martial.[186] In addition, both the prosecution and the defense were permitted one peremptory challenge of anyone except the law member.[187]

For the first time, Congress established a set of personal criteria, as opposed to criteria of rank or branch-of-service, that the convening authority was required to use before appointing panel members:

> When appointing courts-martial the appointing authority shall detail as members thereof those officers of the command who, in his opinion, are best qualified for the duty by reason of age, training, experience, and judicial temperament; and officers having less than two years' service shall not, if it can be avoided without manifest injury to the service, be appointed as members of courts-martial in excess of the minority membership thereof.[188]

These criteria were adopted at the recommendation of Major General Crowder and the War Department.[189] One can argue that they represented a compromise between Ansell's proposal that an independent military judge select panel members and the historic

---

[184] The 1920 Articles gave an accused the right to be represented by either civilian counsel at his own expense or by military counsel if reasonable available. There was not, however, a requirement that the military counsel be an attorney. *See id.* art. 17.

[185] *Id.*

[186] *See id.* art. 50 1/2.

[187] *Id.* art 18.

[188] *Id.* art. 4. Compare this to the modern-day standard, in which the convening authority must consider age, education, training, experience, length of service, and judicial temperament. *See* UCMJ art. 25(d)(2) (2002).

[189] Lamb, *supra* note 22, at 120.

discretionary role of the commander in choosing his own court members. It would remain to be seen whether they were effective.

3. World War II and the Uniform Code of Military Justice: New Statutory Limitations on Convening Authority Discretion

During World War II, the armed services conducted nearly 2,000,000 courts-martial.[190] There had been over one hundred executions, and at war's end, some 45,000 servicemembers were still incarcerated.[191] Some viewed the system as "an instrument of oppression by which officers fortify low-caliber leadership."[192] Concerns about sentence disparity, harsh treatment, and unlawful command influence over the court-martial system produced a strong reform movement that eventually resulted in the Uniform Code of Military Justice.

A post-war clemency board convened by the War Department to review the sentences of servicemembers still in confinement remitted or reduced the sentence in over 85% of the 27,000 cases it reviewed.[193] Secretary of War Patterson appointed an advisory commission to examine the system. The Vanderbilt Committee, as it was known, held full hearings in Washington, D.C, and regional public hearings in New York City, Philadelphia, Baltimore,

---

[190] *Compare* Sherman, *supra* note 54, at 28 (citing a figure of 1,700,000) *with* Lamb, *supra* note 22, at 120 (stating that approximately two million courts-martial were conducted).

[191] Sherman, *supra* note 54, at 27.

[192] Major Gerald F. Crump, *A History of the Structure of Military Justice in the United States, 1921-1966*, 17 A.F. L. REV. 55, 60 (1975), *quoted in* Young, *supra* note 22, at 101.

[193] Sherman, *supra* note 54, at 29.

Raleigh, Atlanta, Chicago, St. Louis, Denver, San Francisco, and Seattle.[194] It did not limit its fact-finding to "the ranks of the malcontent,"[195] but included general officers, enlisted men, volunteer witnesses, the Secretary and Undersecretary of the Army, the Commander of Army Ground Forces, and both The Judge Advocate General and The Assistant Judge Advocate General.[196] The committee found that while the innocent were rarely punished and the guilty rarely set free,[197] there was a serious problem with command domination of the courts-martial system.[198] Committees sponsored by the Department of the Navy reached similar conclusions.[199]

Reform took place in stages. For the Army, Congress passed the Elston Act in 1948.[200] This Act created an independent Judge Advocate General's Corps with a separate promotion list, its own assignment authority, and the guaranteed right for staff judge advocates to communicate to higher echelon staff judge advocates within technical channels.[201] The

---

[194] Farmer & Wels, *supra* note 175, at 265-66.

[195] *Id.* at 266.

[196] Farmer & Wels, *supra* note 175, at 266.

[197] *Id.*

[198] *See* Sherman, *supra* note 54, at 31. In fact, the Committee found that in many instances, the convening authority who appointed the court made a deliberate attempt to influence its decisions. Although not every commander participated in this practice, "its prevalence was not denied and indeed in some instances was freely admitted." REP. WAR DEP'T ADVISORY COMM. MILITARY JUSTICE 6-7 (1946), *quoted in* Farmer & Wels, *supra* note 175, at 268.

[199] Farmer & Wels, note 175, at 266.

[200] The Elston Act is the popular name for the portion of the Selective Service Act of 1948 that amended the Articles of War. *See* Selective Service Act of 1948, Pub. L. No. 80-759, §§ 201-246, 62 Stat. 604, 627-644 (1944) [hereinafter Elston Act].

[201] *See id.* §§ 246-249. *See also* Farmer & Wels, *supra* note 175, at 270.

Elston Act also made changes to court-martial panel composition. For the first time, an enlisted accused was permitted to request trial by a panel consisting of at least one-third enlisted personnel.[202]

The convening authority continued to exercise the discretionary authority to appoint court-martial panel members. In an attempt to solve the problem of unlawful command influence, Congress amended Article of War 88, to prohibit the convening authority and other commanders from censuring, reprimanding, admonishing, coercing, or unlawfully influencing any member in reaching the findings or sentence in any case.[203]

The Elston Act was short-lived. It had no effect on the Navy or Marine Corps, and its applicability to the Air Force, which had become an independent service in 1947, was unclear.[204] In addition, it fell far short of many of the reforms that had been recommended by the various advisory bodies and independent groups. Its main defect, according to bar associations, was that it was a reform in name only, because the commander continued to

---

[202] Elston Act, *supra* note 200, § 203 (amending art. 4 of the Articles of War to grant an enlisted accused the right to have at least one-third of a court-martial panel comprised of enlisted personnel at his written request).

[203] The revised Article 88 prohibited any convening authority or any other commanding officer from censuring, reprimanding, or admonishing a court-martial or any member thereof, "with respect to the findings or sentence adjudged by the court," or with respect to any other exercise by the court or its members of their judicial responsibilities. It also prohibited any person subject to military law from attempting "to coerce or unlawfully influence the action of a court-martial or any military court or commission, or any member thereof," on the findings or sentence of a court-martial. *Id.* § 233 (amending Article of War 88).

[204] Young, *supra* note 22, at 121-22. *But see* Young, *supra* note 22, at 102 (stating that the Elston Act applied to the Army and the Air Force).

exercise the power to appoint the court members, the prosecutor and defense counsel; to refer cases for trial; and to review the findings and sentences of the courts.[205]

Accordingly, the 81st Congress set out to create a unified system of military justice that would apply to all the services, appointing a committee chaired by Harvard Law Professor Edmund Morgan to study military justice and draft appropriate legislation. The Committee made a full study of the law and practices of the different branches of service, the complaints that had been made against the structure and operation of military tribunals, the explanations and answers of service representatives to these complaints, suggestions for reform and service responses as to their practicability, and some provisions of foreign military justice systems.[206]

According to Professor Morgan, the committee's task was to draft legislation that would ensure full protection of the rights of individuals subject to the Code without unduly interfering with either military discipline or the exercise of military functions.[207] This would mean "complete repudiation of a system of military justice conceived of only as an instrument of command" but would also negate "a system designed to be administered as the criminal law is administered in a civilian criminal court."[208] Balancing all these factors, the

---

[205] Farmer & Wels, *supra* note 175, at 273.

[206] Edmund M. Morgan, *The Background of the Uniform Code of Military Justice*, 6 VAND. L. REV. 169, 173 (1952-1953).

[207] *Id.* at 174.

[208] *Id.*

43

committee produced a code that granted unprecedented rights to servicemembers while still retaining command control over the appointment of courts-martial panels.

Both houses of Congress conducted extensive hearings on the Uniform Code of Military Justice.[209] Congress was well aware of the issue of command control, having thoroughly considered testimony on all aspects of the issue. Indeed, the House Committee on Armed Services wrestled considerably with this issue during the hearings, stating in its report, "Perhaps the most troublesome question which we have considered is the question of command control."[210] Some witnesses suggested creating a system in which an independent Judge Advocate General's department would appoint the court from panels submitted by convening authorities.[211] Other witnesses pointed out that a centralized selection process presupposed the constant availability of all members of a panel and could considerably handicap a commander in the discharge of his duties.[212] Mr. Robert W. Smart, a member of the professional staff of the Committee, cut to the heart of the matter when he observed that no matter the system, a clever convening authority who truly wanted to influence a court would find a way to do it in such a way that no one would easily discover

---

[209] *See generally, Hearings on H.R. 2498 Before a Subcomm. of the House Committee on Armed Services*, 81st Cong. (1949), *reprinted in* INDEX AND LEGISLATIVE HISTORY, UNIFORM CODE OF MILITARY JUSTICE (Hein 2000) [hereinafter House Hearings]; *Hearings Before a Subcomm. of the Senate Comm. of Armed Services on S. 857 and H.R.4080*, 81st Cong. (1949), *reprinted in* INDEX AND LEGISLATIVE HISTORY, UNIFORM CODE OF MILITARY JUSTICE (Hein 2000) [hereinafter Senate hearings].

[210] H.R. REP. NO. 81-491, at 7, *reprinted in* INDEX AND LEGISLATIVE HISTORY, UNIFORM CODE OF MILITARY JUSTICE (Hein 2000) [hereinafter House Report].

[211] House Hearings, *supra* note 209, at 648 (prepared statement of Mr. Arthur E. Farmer, Chairman, Committee on Military Law of the War Veterans Bar Association). *See also id.* at 728 (prepared statement of Mr. George A. Spiegelberg, Chairman of the Special Committee on Military Justice of the American Bar Association).

[212] *Id.* at 1124 (statement of Hon. John W. Kenney, Under Secretary of the Navy).

it.[213] Accordingly, "so far as the law is concerned and as far as the Congress can go effectively, all it can do is to express its opposition in good plain words, as here, to such practices."[214]

Ultimately, Congress found that the solution did not lie in removing from commanders the authority to convene courts-martial and appoint court members. According to the House Report

> We fully agree that such a provision [removing the commander from the process] might be desirable if it were practicable, but we are of the opinion that it is not practicable. *We cannot escape the fact that the law which we are now writing will be as applicable and must be as workable in time of war as in time of peace*, and regardless of any desires which may stem from an idealistic conception of justice, we must avoid the enactment of provisions which will unduly restrict those who are responsible for the conduct of our military operations.[215]

The solution, at least according to the House, was to retain the commander's traditional role in convening courts-martial and appointing panel members, while ensuring that appropriate statutory measures were put in place to provide constraints on his power.[216]

---

[213] *Id.* at 1021.

[214] *Id.*

[215] *Id.* at 8 (emphasis added).

[216] The House Report listed several provisions of the UCMJ, that in the Committee's opinion, limited the power of a convening authority: the convening authority could not refer charges for trial until they had been examined for legal sufficiency by the staff judge advocate; the staff judge advocate would be permitted direct communication with the Judge Advocate General; all counsel at general courts-martial were required to be either lawyers or law graduates, certified by the Judge Advocate General; a law officer would play a judicial role at the court-martial, and his rulings on interlocutory questions of law would be final; the staff judge advocate would have to review the record of trial for legal sufficiency before the convening authority could take

Nevertheless, the UCMJ made several changes in the panel-member selection process. First, Article 25 made any member of an armed force eligible to sit on the court-martial of a member of another armed service.[217] Second, warrant officers and enlisted personnel were granted the right to serve on courts-martial panels, and enlisted personnel were guaranteed a panel consisting of at least one-third enlisted upon written request.[218] Third, the qualifications of court members were amended to include "age, education, training, experience, length of service, and judicial temperament."[219] Fourth, UCMJ Article 29, in providing that members of a general or special court-martial could not be absent after

---

action on findings or sentence; the accused would have legally qualified appellate counsel before a board of review and a Court of Military Appeals; the Court of Military Appeals, a civilian appellate court, would preside over the military justice system; and finally, it would be a court-martial offense for any person subject to the Code to unlawfully influence the action of a court-martial. *Id.* at 7-8.

[217] Uniform Code of Military Justice of 1950, art. 25(a), Pub. L. No. 81-506 (codified as amended at 10 U.S.C. §§ 801-946) [hereinafter 1950 UCMJ] ("Any officer on active duty with the armed forces shall be eligible to serve on all courts-martial for the trial of any person who may lawfully be brought before such courts for trial.").

[218] *Id.* art. 25(b), (c)(1). Article 25 stated:

> (b) Any warrant officer on active duty with the armed forces shall be eligible to serve on general and special courts-martial for the trial of any person, other than an officer, who may lawfully be brought before such courts for trial.
>
> (c)(1) Any enlisted person on active duty with the armed forces who is not a member of the same unit as the accused shall be eligible to serve on general and special courts-martial for the trial of any enlisted person who may lawfully be brought before such courts for trial, but he shall serve as a member of the court only if, prior to the convening of such a court, the accused personally has requested in writing that enlisted persons serve on it. After such a request, no enlisted person shall be tried by a general or special court-martial the membership of which does not include enlisted persons in a number comprising at least one-third of the total membership of the court, unless eligible enlisted persons cannot be obtained on account of physical conditions or military exigencies. When such persons cannot be obtained, the court may be convened and the trial held without them, but the convening authority shall make a detailed written statement, to be appended to the record, stating why they could not be obtained.

Id.

[219] *Id.* art. 25(d)(2). This slightly modified the previous requirements under the Articles of War to consider individuals on the basis of age, training, experience, and judicial temperament; with a preference for officers having more than two years' service. *See supra* note 188 and accompanying text.

arraignment without good cause, solved a practice that had existed in the shadowy penumbra of the Articles of War in which convening authorities could reduce or add to the membership of courts-martial panels *during the trial* in an effort to influence the court.[220] Fifth, the UCMJ packed a punch concerning attempts to influence the court. Article 37 prohibited unlawful influence on a court by convening authorities, commanders, or anyone subject to

---

[220] *See* Morgan, *supra* note 206, at 175.

> (a) No member of a general or special court-martial shall be absent or excused after the accused has been arraigned except for physical disability or as a result of challenge or by order of the convening authority for good cause.
>
> (b) Whenever a general court-martial is reduced below five members, the trial shall not proceed unless the convening authority appoints new members sufficient in number to provide not less than five members. When such new members have been sworn, the trial may proceed after the recorded testimony of each witness previously examined has been read to the court in the presence of the law officer, the accused, and counsel.
>
> (c) Whenever a special court-martial is reduced below three members, the trial shall not proceed unless the convening authority appoints new members sufficient in number to provide not less than three members. When such new members have been sworn, the trial shall proceed as if no evidence had been previously introduced, unless a verbatim record of the testimony of previously examined witnesses or a stipulation thereof is read to the court in the presence of the accused and counsel.

1950 UCMJ, *supra* note 217, art. 29.

the Code,[221] while Article 98 made it a punitive offense to knowingly and intentionally violate Article 37.[222]

The UCMJ, then, represented a legislative compromise. It was not an ideal system of justice, but given its purpose of sustaining good order and discipline within the military without unduly impairing operations, it could not be. Over the protests of many individuals, organizations and groups, Congress retained the commander as the central figure of the military justice system, yet significantly modified his powers and added statutory checks and balances to limit outright despotism.

---

[221] Art. 37 provided:

> No authority convening a general, special, or summary court-martial, nor any other commanding officers, shall censure, reprimand, or admonish such court of any member, law officer, or counsel thereof, with respect to the findings or sentence adjudged by the court, or with respect to any other exercise of its or his functions in the conduct of the proceeding. No person subject to this code shall attempt to coerce or, by any unauthorized means, influence the action of a court-martial or any other military tribunal or any member thereof, in reaching the findings or sentence in any case, or the action of any convening, approving, or reviewing authority with respect to his judicial acts.

1950 UCMJ, *supra* note 217, art. 37.

[222] Article 98 provided:

> Any person subject to this code who--

> (1) is responsible for unnecessary delay in the disposition of any case of a person accused of an offense under this code; or

> (2) knowingly and intentionally fails to enforce or comply with any provision of this code regulating the proceedings before, during, or after the trial of an accused;

> shall be punished as a court-martial may direct.

Id. art. 98.

4. 1950 to Present: Continued Oversight and Consistent Rejection of Efforts to Remove Convening Authority from Selection Process

Congress has continued to exercise oversight of the court-martial system. The UCMJ experienced major revisions in 1968[223] and in 1983.[224] Neither of those revisions affected the panel-member selection process.

There have been occasional legislative initiatives to change the panel member selection process, but Congress has not adopted them. In 1971, Senator Birch Bayh of Indiana introduced legislation that would have established an independent court-martial command, the Administrative Division of which would have appointed court-martial members by random selection.[225] Other bills were introduced at about the same time that would have reformed the panel selection system by requiring the convening authority to employ random selection[226] or by requiring the military judge to select the panel using a random selection method.[227] Similar efforts occurred in 1973.[228] In 1983, the Association of the Bar of the

---

[223] *See generally* Military Justice Act of 1968, Pub. L. No. 90-632, 82 Stat. 1335 (1968). Under this Act, the law officer of the earlier code became a full-fledged military judge whose rulings on nearly all interlocutory matters were considered final. *See id.* § 2(9) (amending UCMJ art. 26 to create the position of military judge); *id.* § 2(21) (amending UCMJ art. 51 to permit the military judge to rule on most interlocutory matters). Significantly, the accused was given the option to elect trial by military judge alone. *See id.* § 2(3) (amending UCMJ art. 16 to permit an accused to elect trial by military judge alone in general courts-martial and in special courts-martial to which a military judge had been detailed).

[224] *See generally* Military Justice Act of 1983, Pub. L. No. 98-209, 97 Stat. 1393 (1983).

[225] *See* Birch Bayh, *The Military Justice Act of 1971: The Need for Legislative Reform*, 10 AM. CRIM. L. REV. 9, 13. He introduced S. 1127, 92d Cong., 1st Sess.; 117 CONG. REC. 2550-66 (Mar. 8, 1971).

[226] The Hatfield Bill, S. 4169, 91st Cong., 2d Sess. § 825 (1970), *cited in* Edward F. Sherman, *Congressional Proposals for Reform of Military Law*, 10 AM. CRIM. L. REV. 25 (1971) [Hereinafter Sherman, *Congressional Proposals*].

[227] The Whalen-Price Bill, H.R. 6901, 1st Sess. § 825 (1971); H.R. 2196, 92d Cong. 1st Sess. § 825 (1971), *cited in* Sherman, *Congressional Proposals*, *supra* note 227, at 46.

City of New York launched a campaign to remove the convening authority from panel selection and substitute a system such as random selection.[229] None of these efforts succeeded.

The most recent Congressional action related to panel-member selection was in the 1999 National Defense Authorization Act. Section 552 of the Act required the Secretary of Defense to submit a report on the method of selection of members of the Armed Forces to serve on courts-martial.[230] The Secretary was directed to examine alternatives, including random selection, to the current system of convening authority selection that would be consistent with the "best qualified" criteria of UCMJ Art. 25(d)(2) and solicit input from the Joint Service Committee on Military Justice (JSC).[231]

In its report of 15 August 1999,[232] the JSC explored a number of alternatives to the current selection system, including random nomination, random selection, a combination of random nomination and selection, expanding the source of potential court members, and

---

[228] *See, e.g.*, Kenneth J. Hodson, *Military Justice: Abolish or Change?*, 22 KAN. L. REV. 31 (1973), *reprinted in* Bicentennial Issue, MIL. L. REV. 579, 582 (1975) (discussing bills introduced in the 93d Congress by Senator Bayh and Representative Bennett, and Senator Hatfield).

[229] Lamb, *supra* note 22, at 124-25.

[230] Strom Thurmond National Defense Authorization Act for Fiscal Year 1999, Pub. L. No. 105-261, 112 Stat. 1920.

[231] *Id.* The Joint Service Committee on Military Justice consists of representatives from each of the following officials: the Judge Advocates General of the Army, Navy and Air Force, the Staff Judge Advocate to the Commandant of the Marine Corps, and the Chief Counsel, United States Coast Guard. The JSC's purpose is to assist the President in fulfilling his responsibilities under the UCMJ by conducting an annual review of the MCM and to propose appropriate amendments to the MCM and the UCMJ. *See generally* U.S. DEP'T OF DEFENSE, DIR. 5500.17, ROLE AND RESPONSIBILITIES OF THE JOINT SERVICE COMMITTEE (JSC) ON MILITARY JUSTICE (8 May 1996).

[232] JSC REPORT, *supra* note 29.

using independent selection officials.[233] The JSC concluded that the current system is most likely to obtain "best qualified" members within the operational constraints of the military justice system.[234] Congress has taken no additional action on the matter.

History has shown that Congress has exercised firm control of the military justice system from the Revolution to the present day, before and after the enactment of the Constitution. Over the years, in response to the concerns of its constituents, Congress has made significant changes to the American military justice system. However, despite numerous reform initiatives and proposals, Congress has retained the convening authority's discretionary powers to appoint courts-martial panel members according to statutorily required subjective criteria.

D. The Court-Martial in Context: Legislative Courts and Statutory Due Process

The final step in evaluating the historical and constitutional background of the court-martial is to place it within its proper context as a legislative, or Article I, court. Accordingly, this section will first discuss the Constitutional basis for legislative courts. Next, the section will examine Supreme Court jurisprudence on the Constitutionality of the statutory due process systems Congress has created for some of the other legislative courts. Finally, the section will explore the judicial deference doctrine that the Article III courts apply to issues arising within courts-martial.

---

[233] *Id.* at 3.

[234] *Id.*

1. Introduction to Legislative Courts

Article III of the Constitution states that "[t]he judicial Power of the United States, shall be vested in one supreme Court, and in such inferior Courts as the Congress may from time to time ordain and establish."[235] The hallmark of these courts is the judicial independence provided by the life tenure and salary guarantees of Article III, section 1.[236] Article III courts include the Supreme Court, the Circuit Courts of Appeal, and the United States District Courts.[237]

The Article III courts, however, do not handle all the judicial business of the United States. For over two hundred years, Congress has used its enumerated powers under the Constitution in conjunction with the Necessary and Proper clause[238] to create specialized tribunals,[239] including courts-martial,[240] that are free from the tenure and salary protections of

---

[235] U.S. CONST. art. III, § 1.

[236] Section 1 provides that the judges "shall hold their Offices during good Behaviour, and shall, at stated times, receiver for their Services, a Compensation, which shall not be diminished during their Continuance in Office." *Id.*

[237] *See* LAURENCE H. TRIBE, AMERICAN CONSTITUTIONAL LAW § 3-5, at 43 (2d ed. 1988).

[238] U.S. CONST. art. I, § 8, cl. 18 ("To make all Laws which shall be necessary and proper for carrying into Execution the foregoing powers, and all other Powers vested by this Constitution in the Government of the United States, or in any Department or Officer thereof.").

[239] Examples of these courts include the territorial courts, subject to Congressional governance under Article IV of the Constitution; the District of Columbia court system, created pursuant to Congress's Article I authority to exercise exclusive legislation over the District of Columbia; the consular courts, which stemmed from Congress's power over treaties and foreign commerce; the Tax Court, rooted in the power to "lay and collect taxes"; and, of course, the courts-martial system, created pursuant to Congress's authority to provide rules for the government of the land and naval forces. *See* Richard B. Saphire and Michael E. Solimine, *Shoring Up Article III: Legislative Court Doctrine in the Post* CFTC v. Schor *Era,* 68 B.U. L. REV. 85, 89-91 (1988). There have also been, over the years, a number of other tribunals formed for limited purposes, including the Court for Chinal, the Court of Private Land Claims, the Choctaw & Chickasaw Citizenship Court, and the Court of Customs Appeals. *See* Ex Parte Bakelite Corp., 279 U.S. 438, 450-458 (1929) (listing the various legislative courts).

Article III.[241] Although these courts use the judicial process in adjudicating cases,[242] they do not partake of the 'judicial power of the United States' within the meaning of Article III.[243] The Supreme Court has occasionally struggled to define the proper limits of legislative courts,[244] but there is no Constitutional infirmity in Congress's creation and operation of them.[245] In fact, there are sound pragmatic reasons for these courts--among them flexibility and ease of administration--and the Supreme Court has accorded considerable deference to

---

[240] *See* U.S. CONST. art. I, § 8, cl. 14. *See also* Dynes v. Hoover, 61 U.S. (20 How.) 65, 79 (1858) (stating that the power for Congress to provide for the trial and punishment of army and navy personnel "is given without any connection between it and the 3d article of the Constitution defining the judicial power of the United States").

[241] *See* Paul M. Bator, *The Constitution as Architecture: Legislative and Administrative Courts Under Article III*, 65 IND. L. J. 233, 235 (1990); *see also* 15 JAMES WM. MOORE ET AL., MOORE'S FEDERAL PRACTICE § 100.40 (3d ed. 1999).

[242] *See, e.g.,* Craig A. Stern, *What's a Constitution Among Friends?--Unbalancing Article III*, 146 U. PA. L. REV. 1043, 1055 (1998).

[243] *See, e.g.,* American Ins. Co. v. Canter, 26 U.S. (1 Pet.) 511, 546 (1828). In *Canter*, Chief Justice Marshall made a famous statement about the relationship of the legislative courts to the judicial power of the nation.

> These Courts, then, are not constitutional Courts, in which the judicial power conferred by the Constitution on the general government can be deposited. They are incapable of receiving it. They are legislative Courts, created in virtue of the general right of sovereignty which exists in the government, or in virtue of that clause which enables Congress to make all needful rules and regulations respecting the territory belonging to the United States. The jurisdiction with which they are invested, is not a part of that judicial power which is defined in the 3d article of the Constitution, but is conferred by Congress.

Id.

[244] *See generally* Stern, *supra* note 242 (reviewing legislative court doctrine and suggesting that the text of the Constitution permits courts-martial, territorial courts, adjudication of public rights, and creation of judicial adjuncts without infringing on art. III); Bator, *supra* note 241 (discussing the Court's legislative courts jurisprudence, criticizing it, and suggesting a framework in which Article III tribunals provide review of the legal and factual determinations of art. I courts); Saphire & Solomine, *supra* note 239 (discussing the Court's jurisprudence on the matter and criticizing the balancing test of *Commodity Futures Trading Co. v. Schor*, 478 U.S. 833 (1986)).

[245] *See* Saphire & Solomine, *supra* note 239, at 89.

Congress in "the choice of means it thought 'necessary and proper' to implement the powers explicitly delegated to it under the Constitution."[246]

Legislative courts play a useful role in assisting Congress efficiently to carry out its enumerated powers, particularly when the use of "full-blown 'national' tribunals with judges enjoying life tenure and restricted to a 'judiciary' power has seemed awkward and inappropriate in the context of meeting certain other adjudicatory needs."[247] Courts-martial are a prime example of a court system where the protections, procedures, and inherent inefficiencies of the Article III courts would interfere with the military's ability to effectively use the system to help maintain good order and discipline. "Thus, from the beginning," wrote Paul Bator, a law professor at the University of Indiana, "soldiers and sailors have been tried by military tribunals administering a specialized military justice."[248]

2. Fundamental Rights, Statutory Due Process and the Legislative Courts

Even when life and liberty are at stake, legislative courts are not required to grant due process rights that are intrinsic to the Article III courts.[249] The Supreme Court has, instead, employed an analysis that examines whether the statutory due process system of a given legislative court grants what it calls "fundamental rights." This section will analyze the

---

[246] Saphire and Solimine, *supra* note 239, at 89.

[247] Bator, *supra* note 241, at 235.

[248] *Id.*

[249] *See, e.g.*, Curry v. Sec'y of the Army, 595 F.2d 873 (D.C. Cir. 1979) ("We agree that the system established in the UCMJ would be inconsistent with due process if instituted in the context of a civilian criminal trial.").

Supreme Court's treatment of statutory due process systems in the consular and territorial court systems.

a. Consular Courts

The consular courts arose from Congress's authority over treaties and commerce under the Article I of the Constitution.[250] Under this system, American ministers and consuls were granted extensive power over U.S. citizens pursuant to U.S. treaty obligations.[251] Congress established a statutory system in which the minister and consuls of the United States in certain overseas locations[252] were invested with judicial authority and could arraign and try all citizens of the United States charged with offenses of host-country law.[253] The consular courts had neither grand juries nor petit juries.

The leading case on the consular courts is *In Re Ross*.[254] The appellant, a British seaman serving on an American merchant ship in Japan, was tried for murder and sentenced to death by a consular court consisting of the consul and four associates.[255] The appellant filed a writ

---

[250] U.S. CONST. art. I, § 8, cl. 1; *see also* Saphire & Solomine, *supra* note 239, at 90.

[251] *See* MOORE, *supra* note 241, at § 100 app.02[7].

[252] Japan, China, Siam, and Madagascar. *See In re* Ross, 140 U.S. 453 (1891).

[253] Rev. Stat. §§ 4083-4096 (1878).

[254] 140 U.S. 453 (1891). The appellant in *In re Ross* was represented by counsel and filed several motions with the consular court, including a motion for grand jury presentment and a motion for a trial by petit jury. All of the motions were denied. His death sentence was approved by the United States minister in Japan, but it was commuted to life in prison by the President of the United States. *Id.* at 453-61.

[255] This was pursuant to Revised Statutes § 4106 (1878), which required a consul to sit with a panel of four for capital cases. The method of selection was a modified form of random selection, in which the associates, as

of habeas corpus in the Circuit Court for the Northern District of New York, alleging that he had been denied his Fifth Amendment right to grand jury presentment and his Sixth Amendment right to trial by petit jury. The Circuit Court denied the writ, and on appeal, the Supreme Court affirmed.[256]

In affirming the denial of the writ, the Court first noted the centuries-old existence of consular courts as a means by which nations could protect their citizens from the hostile and alien forms of justice practiced in the "non-Christian" nations.[257] It held that the statutory framework for the consular courts, despite its failure to provide for grand jury presentment or trial by petit jury, did not violate the Constitution because the Constitution did not have extraterritorial application.[258] Finally, it examined the due process rights actually afforded to the appellant and concluded that under the consular court system granted the appellant had "the benefit of all the provisions necessary to secure a fair trial before the consul and his associates": the opportunity to examine the complaint against him, the right to confront and cross-examine the witnesses against him, and representation by counsel.[259]

---

they were called, were "taken by lot from a list which had previously been submitted to and approved by the minister." *Id.* The only requirement was that they be "Persons of good repute and competent for the duty." *Id.*

[256] *Ross*, 140 U.S. at 480.

[257] *Id.* at 462-63.

[258] *Id.* at 464.

[259] *Id.* at 470.

The *In re Ross* holding that the Constitution had no extraterritorial applicability was effectively overruled in *Reid v. Covert*,[260] when the Court stated that *In re Ross* "rested, at least in substantial part, on a fundamental misconception" and "should be left as a relic from a different era."[261] Nonetheless, the *In re Ross* analysis of what constitutes a fair trial-- notice, the right of confrontation, and the assistance of counsel--has never been overruled.[262]

b. The Territorial Courts

Article IV of the Constitution grants Congress the power to "make all needful Rules and Regulations respecting the Territory or other Property belonging to the United States."[263] As part of this power, Congress has established legislative courts to handle both criminal and civil matters within the territories. The Supreme Court has upheld creation of these courts based on the perception "that the Framers intended that as to certain geographical areas, in which no State operated as sovereign, Congress was to exercise the general powers of government."[264] In its role as a sovereign power over the territories, Congress assumes a role similar to a state or municipal government and is not bound by the tenure and salary restrictions of Article III. The same analysis applies to the District of Columbia, in which

---

[260] In *Reid v. Covert*, 345 U.S. 1 (1957), the Court invalidated a statutory grant of courts-martial jurisdiction over persons accompanying the armed forces overseas, holding that the

[261] 345 U.S. 1, 12 (1957).

[262] *Cf.* United States v. Verdugo-Urquidez, 494 U.S. 259, 277 (1990) (Kennedy, J., concurring) (noting that the Court has never overruled *In re Ross*).

[263] U.S. CONST. art. IV, § 3.

[264] *Northern Pipeline Construction Co.*, 458 U.S. at 64.

Congress "has entire control over the district for every purpose of government,"[265] including the courts.

Doctrinally, the Supreme Court has divided the territories into two types, incorporated territories and the District of Columbia, and unincorporated territories such as Puerto Rico or the Virgin Islands.[266] The extent to which due process rights apply depends on the status of the territories. In the incorporated territories and the District of Columbia, criminal defendants have no right to be tried before an independent judiciary with the tenure and salary protections of Article III.[267] The inhabitants of these areas are, however, entitled to grand jury presentment according to the Fifth Amendment and trial by petit jury according to the Sixth Amendment.[268]

---

[265] Kendall v. United States, 12 Pet. 524, 619 (1838).

[266] An incorporated territory is one in which the treaty of cession or agreement by which the United States acquired the territory specifically manifests an intent to incorporate the territory in the United States. An unincorporated territory, in contrast, is one in which the treaty of cession or acquisition agreement does not manifest such an intent. *See* Dorr v. United States, 195 U.S. 138, 143 (1904). At the turn of the century, the Philippines and Puerto Rico were unincorporated territories that had been obtained by a treaty of cession from Spain. *See* Carlos R. Soltero, *The Supreme Court Should Overrule the Territorial Incorporation Doctrine and End One Hundred Years of Judicially Condoned Colonialism*, 22 CHICANO-LATINO L. REV. 1, 6 (2001). In 1917, the United States purchased the Virgin Islands from Denmark, and those islands became an unincorporated territory. *See* Joycelyn Hewlett, *The Virgin Islands: Grand Jury Denied*, 35 HOW. L. J. 263, 265 (1992). The Philippines are now an independent nation, but Puerto Rico and the Virgin Islands remain unincorporated territories of the United States to this day.

[267] *See* RONALD J. ROTUNDA & JOHN E. NOWAK, 1 TREATISE ON CONSTITUTIONAL LAW: SUBSTANCE AND PROCEDURE § 3.11 (3d ed. 1999).

[268] In *Callan v. Wilson*, 127 U.S. 540, 550 (1888), the Court ruled on a challenge to a District of Columbia law that gave original jurisdiction of certain offenses to a police court. In striking down this provision, the Court stated that there was "nothing in the history of the Constitution or of the original amendments to justify the assertion that the people of this District may be lawfully deprived of the benefit of any of the constitutional guarantees of life, liberty, and property -- especially of the privilege of trial by jury in criminal cases." In its analysis, the Court noted that right of trial by jury had always been interpreted to apply to the occupants of the territories and stated, "We cannot think that the people of this District have, in that regard, less rights than those accorded to the people of the Territories of the United States." *Id.*

The unincorporated territories are somewhat different. In a line of cases dating back to the early twentieth century, the Supreme Court has ruled that the full protections of the Constitution do not extend to these areas. In *Dorr v. United States*,[269] the Court addressed the issue of whether Congress was Constitutionally required to legislatively provide for trial by jury in the Philippines.[270] Relying on the Insular cases,[271] the Court held that because the Philippines were an unincorporated territory, the full protections of the Constitution did not apply to the inhabitants.[272] Congress was bound by the specific limitations imposed by the Constitution on its power, such as the prohibition against *ex post facto* laws or bills of attainder, but otherwise had only to provide fundamental rights in the unincorporated territories.[273] Citing prior decisions, the Court stated that trial by jury and presentment by grand jury were not fundamental rights.[274]

---

[269] 195 U.S. 138 (1904). The petitioners in *Dorr* were newspaper editors accused of committing libel in the Philippines. At trial, they demanded indictment by grand jury and trial by petit jury, both of which were denied because they were not required under Filipino law. They appealed to the Supreme Court of the Philippines and from there to the United States Supreme Court. *Id.*

[270] When the Philippines came under United States control, Congress established a criminal justice system based on the civil law that had governed the Philippines under Spanish rule for several hundred years. The system did not include trial by jury. *Id.* at 145.

[271] The Insular cases developed the doctrine of territorial incorporation. They were not criminal cases, but rather were challenges based on the Uniformity Clause of the Constitution, U.S. CONST. art. 1, § 8, to duties imposed on commercial goods exchanged between the territories and the United States. *Downes v. Bidwell*, 182 U.S. 244 (1901), was the most important of these cases. It held that the Uniformity Clause did not apply to the territories. It also made the distinction between incorporated and unincorporated territories and the reach of the Constitution in both. *See* Soltero, *supra* note 266, at 150.

[272] *Dorr*, 195 U.S. at 149.

[273] *Id.* at 145-48.

[274] *Id.*

The Court then analyzed the Filipino statutory due process system, in which an accused was given the right of counsel, to demand the nature and cause of the accusation against him, to have a speedy and public trial, to confront the witnesses against him, compulsory process of witnesses, due process, prohibition against double jeopardy, the privilege against self-incrimination, and appellate rights.[275] Writing for the majority, Justice Day stated, "It cannot be successfully maintained that this system does not give an adequate and efficient method of protecting the rights of the accused as well as executing the criminal law by judicial proceedings, which give full opportunity to be heard by competent tribunals before judgment can be pronounced."[276]

A few years later, the Court elaborated on the formula it had established in *Dorr* in another newspaper libel case, this time from Puerto Rico. In *Balzac v. People of Porto Rico* [sic],[277] the appellant had been tried for misdemeanor libel in a Puerto Rican court. The Puerto Rican code of criminal procedure at the time permitted jury trial for felony cases but not misdemeanor cases.[278] The appellant argued that the statute violated his Constitutional right to trial by jury. The Court disagreed, ruling that Puerto Rico was not an incorporated territory within the meaning of its prior jurisprudence.[279] Thus, the full protections of the

---

[275] *Id.* at 145-46.

[276] *Id.*

[277] 258 U.S. 298 (1921).

[278] *Id.* at 302-03.

[279] The appellant argued that he was entitled to the full protections of the Constitution because of the Jones Act of 1917, which granted United States citizenship to residents of Puerto Rico who did not opt out within six months. The Jones Act contained a section entitled the "Bill of Rights," which gave every one of the constitutional guarantees to the Puerto Ricans *except* indictment by grand jury and trial by petit jury. *Id.* at 306-

Constitution did not apply there as a matter of right; due process rights such as grand jury presentment or trial by petit jury could only be granted statutorily.[280]

The Court again applied its fundamental rights analysis from *Dorr*. It defined fundamental rights as "those . . . personal rights declared in the Constitution, as for instance that no person could be deprived of life, liberty or property without due process of law,"[281] but, quoting *Dorr*, stated that trial by jury was not a fundamental right. The Court focused on Congress's power to govern the territories under Article IV, § 3 and the fact that even as Congress provided a Bill of Rights for the Puerto Ricans, it excluded grand and petit juries.[282]

The holdings in *Dorr* and *Balzac* are still valid.[283] While they do not apply *per se* to courts-martial, they do illustrate that the Court applies a different Constitutional analysis to legislative courts than to Article III courts. Even in matters affecting life and liberty, no litigant in legislative court enjoys the benefits of an independent judiciary with tenure and salary protections. Furthermore, rights such as grand jury presentment and trial by petit jury

---

07. The Supreme Court disagreed with the appellant's theory. Carefully parsing the Jones Act, the Court found nothing in it to demonstrate a Congressional intent to incorporate Puerto Rico into the Union. *Id.* at 307-08.

[280] By the time the case reached the Supreme Court, the Puerto Rican legislature had amended its code to statutorily permit trial by jury in misdemeanor cases. *Id.* at 303.

[281] *Id.* at 312-13.

[282] *See id.* at 306-07, 312.

[283] *See, e.g.*, Soltero, *supra* note 266, at 4 (noting that in recent decisions, the Rehnquist court has upheld the validity of these cases); *see also* United States v. Verdugo-Urquidez, 494 U.S. 259, 268 (1990) (favorably discussing Insular cases and their progeny as still-valid precedent); De La Rosa v. United States, 229 F.3d 80, 87 (3d Cir. 2000) (noting that the "fundamental rights" doctrine of *Balzac* and *Dorr* still applies to Puerto Rico today).

that would be Constitutionally required in Article III courts may not be required in all legislative courts. Where Congress acts pursuant to its enumerated Constitutional powers and in accordance with valid Congressional aims, a statutory form of due process that guarantees a fair trial and fundamental rights is sufficient.

Fundamental rights as defined in these cases include the right for an accused to know the nature of the charges against him, assistance of counsel, right of confrontation, privilege against self-incrimination, speedy trial, compulsory process of witnesses, protection against double jeopardy, the right to appeal, and due process of law before a competent tribunal.

3. Courts-Martial and the Military Deference Doctrine

a. Introduction to the Doctrine

Of all the legislative courts created by Congress, courts-martial have received the most deference from the Article III courts. Under a standard of review known as the "separate community"[284] or "military deference"[285] doctrine, the courts have proclaimed the armed forces to be a distinct subculture with unique needs, "a specialized society separate from

---

[284] *See generally* James M. Hirshhorn, *The Separate Community: Military Uniqueness and Servicemen's Constitutional Rights*, 62 N.C. L. REV. 177 (1984) (providing a theoretical framework and justification for the military deference doctrine).

[285] *See generally* John F. O'Connor, *The Origins and Application of the Military Deference Doctrine*, 35 GA. L. REV. 161 (2000). O'Connor notes that the doctrine has developed in three stages during our country's history. During the first stage, which lasted until the mid-1950's, there was virtually no meaningful constitutional review of military regulations and procedures. The second stage featured an activist court that sought to curtail what it viewed as Congress's inappropriate attempts to extend courts-martial jurisdiction; the stage ended with the *O'Callahan v. Parker* decision, which established the service connection test. The third stage was the development of the military deference doctrine as we know it, beginning in the mid 1970s. *Id.*

civilian society."[286] Where there is a conflict between the Constitutional rights of the individual serviceman and an asserted military purpose, the courts have deferred to Congress's ability--indeed, duty--to balance the appropriate factors and reach a necessary compromise.[287]

This doctrine is firmly rooted in the principle of separation of powers. The Supreme Court has stated that individual rights of servicemembers "must perforce be conditioned to meet certain overriding demands of discipline and duty, and the civil courts are not the agencies which must determine the precise balance to be struck in this adjustment. The Framers expressly entrusted that task to Congress."[288] In furtherance of that duty, the Constitution does not impose limits on Congress, but rather empowers it.[289]

The Courts defer to Congressional judgment on matters of good order and discipline because the military's mission to fight and win the nation's wars is different from any other activity of the government. In order for the military to carry out its duties properly, it must

---

[286] Parker v. Levy, 417 U.S. 733, 743 (1974).

[287] Id.

[288] Burns v. Wilson, 346 U.S. 137, 140 (1953). In Burns, the petitioners were tried separately by Air Force courts-martial and convicted of murder and rape on the island of Guam. At trial, they raised a number of issues pertaining to their treatment by Guam authorities, their confessions, and the trial procedures at the courts-martial. They exhausted their remedies through the military court system and then applied for a writ of habeas corpus in the United States District Court for the District of Columbia. Id. at 138. The district court denied the writ, and both the Court of Appeal and the Supreme Court affirmed. Id. at 137. The Supreme Court held that because Congress had established a separate justice system for the military with its own system of review, the civil courts would limit their review of a habeas corpus petition to determining whether the military courts had given fair consideration to the petitioner's claims at trial. Id. at 144.

[289] See Hirshhorn, supra note 284, at 211.

be subordinate to the political will, and it must be internally disciplined.[290] The very survival

of the nation is at stake. Therefore, the consequences of judicial error concerning the effect

of a practice on military effectiveness are particularly serious.[291]

The modern servicemember, whether an infantryman engaged in direct combat or a

rear-echelon administrative specialist, must be able to perform effectively while beyond the

direct supervision of officers.[292] Adherence to group standards is necessary for the

fulfillment of unpleasant duties that the typical member of society does not have to face.[293]

The existence of formal disciplinary authority is critical in maintaining this capability. As

the Supreme Court stated in *Schlesinger v. Councilman*,[294] "To prepare for and perform its

vital role, the military must insist upon a respect for duty and a discipline without counterpart

---

[290] *See id.* at 219-21. Hirshhorn explains that good order and discipline is particularly significant in a system subordinates the military to civilian leadership:

> As long as the Constitution gives the President and Congress the authority to determine the ends for which military force will be used, civilian supremacy requires a system of military discipline that inculcates all ranks with an attitude of active subordination, i.e., the will to carry out the instructions of their civilian superiors despite their own disagreement.

Id. at 217.

[291] *Id.* at 239. The consequences of insubordination or indiscipline can be devastating to national policies. Hirshhorn cites McClellan's attempt to control Lincoln's policy on slavery by threatening that his troops would not fight for emancipation and the 1914 action of British officers in preventing Home Rule for Ireland by threatening to resign en masse rather than fight the Ulster Protestants. *Id.* at 217.

[292] *Id.* at 221.

[293] *Cf. id.* at 225-26 (discussing the importance of soldiers internalizing the values of their larger military group in order to carry out the unpleasant duties of combat, as well as less dangerous duties in rear-echelon areas).

[294] 420 U.S. 738 (1975).

in civilian life."[295] In other words, servicemembers must believe that the military has the power to detect and punish resistance or noncompliance with its standards.[296]

In discharging its Constitutional function of making rules for the government of the armed forces, Congress has balanced the laws, interests, and traditions of the military with the rights of individual servicemembers.[297] Thus, the Article III courts are conscious of the consequences of judicial miscalculation concerning the effect of individual rights on military efficiency. Because the political branches have, in acting, already weighed the affected individual interests, any judicial decision that constitutionalizes the individual interests of the servicemember rejects the balance struck by Congress.[298]

b. Application to the UCMJ's Statutory Due Process Framework

The statutory due process system of the UCMJ is Constitutionally acceptable within its context, although some of the same procedures (for example, the practice of a convening authority using subjective criteria to personally select members of the court) would be Constitutionally infirm in an Article III court.[299] In his concurring opinion in *Weiss v. United*

---

[295] *Id.* at 757.

[296] *See* Hirshhorn, *supra* note 284, at 224-27.

[297] *Schlesinger*, 420 U.S. at 757.

[298] *See* Hirshhorn, *supra* note 284, at 231.

[299] *See* O'Connor, *supra* note 285, at 161 ("At the risk of oversimplification, the military deference doctrine requires that a court considering certain constitutional challenges to military legislation perform a more lenient constitutional review than would be appropriate if the challenged legislation were in the civilian context.").

States,[300] Justice Scalia captured the essence of the matter, observing that Congress had achieved due process within the meaning of the Due Process Clause[301] when it set up a framework to give procedural protection to servicemembers.[302] "That is enough," he wrote, "and to suggest otherwise arrogates to this Court a power it does not possess."[303]

The statutory due-process framework of the courts-martial system, as a legislative court, differs considerably from the Article III courts. As with all legislative courts, there is no requirement for an independent judiciary with tenure and salary protections; it is enough that the UCMJ and military regulations effectively insulate them from unlawful command influence.[304] It has long been settled that the rights of grand jury presentment and trial by petit jury do not apply to courts-martial.[305] The Sixth Amendment right to assistance of counsel is not required at summary courts-martial.[306] As for actual court composition, the

[300] 510 U.S. 163 (1994). In *Weiss*, the Court addressed the issue of whether the appellant's convictions violated due process because the military judge had been appointed in violation of the Appointments Clause and because the lack of a fixed term of office for military judges violated the Due Process Clause. The Court held that military judges, as officers, had already been properly appointed and did not require a separate appointment under the Appointments Clause. The Court noted that the Constitution does not require life tenure for Article I judges, but that the statutory and regulatory protections in place provided adequate due process protections for servicemembers. *Id.* at 166-179.

[301] "Nor shall [any person] . . . be deprived of life, liberty, or property, without due process of law." U.S. CONST. amend. V.

[302] *See Weiss*, 510 U.S. at 197 (Scalia, J., concurring).

[303] *Id.*

[304] *See id.* at 176-77.

[305] *See, e.g, Ex parte* Quirin, 317 U.S. 1, 40 (1942) (stating that cases arising in the land and naval forces are excluded from grand jury indictment by the Fifth Amendment and excluded by implication from the Sixth); *Ex parte* Milligan, 71 U.S. (4 Wall) 2, 123 (stating that the Framers intended to limit the Sixth Amendment trial by jury to those who were subject to indictment by the Fifth Amendment).

[306] Middendorf v. Henry, 425 U.S. 25 (1976). A summary court-martial is a one-man court in which neither the prosecution nor the defense is permitted representation by counsel. For certain grades of enlisted soldiers, the maximum penalty is up to thirty days' incarceration. A soldier who objects to trial by summary court-martial

Supreme Court has stated that this is a matter appropriate for Congressional action.[307] Lower courts have rejected the idea that convening authority selection of panel members somehow violates due process, noting that Congress deliberately continued the historical scheme of convening authority panel member selection despite strong objections to the process.[308]

The accused in a court-martial enjoys due process rights that are similar to the fundamental rights the Court recognized in the consular and insular cases.[309] He has the right to assistance of counsel at all levels of court-martial except the summary court,[310] to be informed of the charges against him,[311] to a speedy trial,[312] to compulsory process of witnesses and evidence,[313] to the privilege against self-incrimination,[314] to extensive

---

may demand trial by a higher level of court-martial (with greater due process rights and greater punishment potential) as a matter of right. *See* UCMJ art. 20 (2002).

[307] Whelchel v. McDonald, 340 U.S. 122 (1950). The petitioner was convicted of raping a German woman. He argued that, although the Articles of War at the time did not permit enlisted men to serve on courts-martial panels, he was entitled to have them. The Court stated that he could

> gain no support from the analogy of trial by jury in the civil courts. The right to trial by jury guaranteed in the Sixth Amendment is not applicable to trials by courts-martial or military commissions. . . . The constitution of courts-martial, like other matters relating to their organization and administration, is a matter appropriate for congressional action.

Id. at 126-27 (citations omitted).

[308] McDonald v. United States, 531 F.2d 490, 493 (Ct. Cl. 1976).

[309] *See generally supra* Part II.D.2.

[310] UCMJ art. 27 (2002) (providing for the detail of trial and defense counsel to general and special courts-martial).

[311] *Id.* art. 35 (establishing procedures for serving the charges on an accused and guaranteeing that he cannot be tried for a certain period of time thereafter (5 days for a general court-martial and 3 days for a special court-martial) over his objection).

[312] MCM, *supra* note 5, R.C.M. 707 (requiring that an accused be brought to trial within 120 days after preferral of charges, imposition of pretrial restraint, or entry on active duty for the purpose of trial).

[313] UCMJ art. 46 (2002) (guaranteeing equal opportunity to obtain witnesses and evidence).

appellate rights.[315] In short, the UCMJ ensures that a military accused receives due process of law before a competent and impartial tribunal.[316]

When placed into its proper context as a legislative court formed in furtherance of a Constitutionally enumerated Congressional power, the statutory grant of due process in a court-martial compares quite favorably with what a criminal accused can demand as a matter of right in the other legislative courts. The balance that Congress has struck will not lightly be disturbed by an Article III court.[317]

---

[314] *Id.* art. 31.

[315] *See generally* UCMJ art. 60 (2002) (empowering the convening authority to grant clemency on findings or sentence); *id.* art. 66 (establishing service courts of criminal appeals); *id.* art. 67 (providing for review by a civilian Court of Appeals for the Armed Forces); *id* art. 67a (granting the right for an accused to seek review from the Supreme Court by writ of certiorari).

[316] *See, e.g.,* United States v. Modesto, 43 M.J. 315, 318 (1995) (stating that the "sine qua non for a fair court-martial" is impartial panel members and noting the variety of procedural safeguards in the military justice system to ensure the impartiality of the members).

[317] *Cf.* Middendorf v. Henry, 425 U.S. 25, 44 (1976) (noting, with respect to summary courts-martial, that Congress had twice entertained and rejected proposals to eliminate them; therefore, it would take extraordinarily weighty factors to upset the balance struck by Congress). On at least three occasions, Congress considered and rejected proposals to eliminate the convening authority's role in panel member selection, each time apparently concluding that retaining the process maintained a proper balance between individual rights and Congress's power to govern and regulate the armed forces. *See supra* Part II.C.4 (discussing Congressional oversight of the UCMJ since 1950 and discussing reform proposals that would have eliminating the convening authority from the panel selection process).

III. Analysis of Attacks on Convening Authority Appointment of Panel Members

The beginning of wisdom in the law is the ability to make distinctions, to withstand the reductionist pressure to say that one thing must necessarily lead to another.[318]

Current reform efforts attack the role of the convening authority on three broad theoretical fronts. The first front seeks to blur the distinction between courts-martial panels and juries as a means to imposing random panel-member selection on the military justice system. The second front takes an internationalist bent, arguing that because Great Britain and Canada, whose military justice systems share a common heritage with ours in the British Articles of War, have removed the convening authority from panel selection, so should we. The third front is fought in the courtroom by a bare majority of the CAAF, who have judicially legislated a significant modification to UCMJ Article 25(d)(2) using a weapon of their own creation, an implied bias doctrine that substitutes judicial speculation for the measured fact-finding and deliberation of Congress. This section will examine each of these attacks in turn.

A. Random Selection and the Application of the Jury-Selection Template to Courts-Martial

1. The Strategy: Blur the Lines Between Juries and Courts-Martial

Reform efforts that have random selection as their ultimate goal often employ a strategy that blurs the lines between court-martial panel selection and jury selection. While nominally

---

[318] Bator, *supra* note 241, at 263.

accepting the axiom that the Sixth Amendment jury trial right does not exist at courts-martial, these efforts nevertheless engraft the doctrines and principles of the Supreme Court's jury selection jurisprudence onto the courts-martial system, claiming that random selection is a necessary antecedent to due process and the only way truly to avoid unlawful command influence.

A prime example of this strategy is an article, *Courts-Martial and the Commander*,[319] published over 30 years ago by Major General Kenneth J. Hodson, a section of which is devoted to reforming the court-martial panel selection process. The underlying premise of General Hodson's argument is that convening authority selection of panel members is undesirable because it is either actually unfair or presents the appearance of evil.[320] To solve the problem, he suggests using the Supreme Court's jury selection jurisprudence as a template for the military justice system.

Terminology is the first thing to fall as the article loosely interchanges the nomenclature of the jury and the court-martial panel.[321] The goals of the systems are confounded next. Citing seminal Supreme Court cases[322] and the ABA Standards for Criminal Justice,[323] the

---

[319] Hodson, *supra* note 22.

[320] Hodson recognizes that the UCMJ provides remedies for unlawful command influence but says it is not good enough: "The military system has the appearance of evil and the potential for abuse." *Id.* at 64.

[321] *See, e.g., id.* at 60 ("the military jury differs from the civilian jury in that it almost always consists of less than twelve members"); *id.* at 64 ("The members of a court-martial (the military jury) are selected by the commander.").

[322] The article quotes *Williams v. Florida*, 399 U.S. 78, 100 (1970) for the idea that the essential feature of a jury is "the interposition between the accused and his accuser of the commonsense judgment of a group of layman, and in the community participation and shared responsibility that results from the group's determination of guilt or innocence." Hodson, *supra* note 22, at 61. This is significantly different from the

article defines the goal of the jury system as "random selection from a cross-section of the community,"[324] an unexceptionable conclusion. The article next transfers this goal--lock, stock, and barrel--to the military justice system: "Given the goal of random selection from a cross-section of the community, the present law which allows the commander to select military jurors, and even to exclude enlisted men unless they are requested by the accused, should be changed."[325] The article suggests a form of random selection in which the military judge would solicit names from the units in his judicial district and use a jury wheel to draw names for trial.[326] Finally, the analysis of the proposed system almost entirely glosses over the effects random selection might have on the operational effectiveness of the military justice system in both peace and war.[327]

---

military tradition of a panel of professionals who judge an accused based on the facts and decide based not only on common sense, but also on the principles of military law and their shared sense of the demands of good order and discipline.

[323] Hodson, *supra* note 22, at 62, 64 (quoting ABA PROJECT ON MINIMUM STANDARDS FOR CRIMINAL JUSTICE, STANDARDS RELATING TO TRIAL BY JURY, § 2.1(a) at 48-51).

[324] Hodson, *supra* note 22, at 64.

[325] *Id.* It is interesting that the modern-day ABA standards relating to jury trials specifically note that they do not apply to the procedures of military justice tribunals. AMERICAN BAR ASSOCIATION, ABA STANDARDS FOR CRIMINAL JUSTICE: DISCOVERY AND TRIAL BY JURY (3d ed. 1996), Standard 15-1.1(d) [hereinafter ABA STANDARDS], *available at* http://www.abanet.org/crimjust/standards/jurytrial_toc.html.

[326] Hodson, *supra* note 22.

[327] The article proposes presumptively disqualifying the lowest two or three enlisted grades, using a questionnaire to help streamline the voir dire process, and providing discretion for the judge to excuse those who are unavailable because of their duties. It does not discuss in any detail the process by which the commands within the proposed judicial districts would submit names to the military judge or how improper command influence would be avoided in that process. The article entirely fails to analyze the effect such a random selection system might have in a deployed or combat environment. It focuses on the administration of a justice system to the almost entire exclusion of addressing the unique issues of a military justice system. *See generally, id.* at 64-65.

With relatively minor exceptions, the various attacks on panel member selection for the past thirty years generally follow the analytical template established by this article. The starting point is almost always the premise that command control of the court-martial selection process is either actually evil or presents the appearance thereof.[328] Next, the indiscriminate interchange of terminology and concepts[329] prepares the way for the interesting but inapposite historical discussion of the common law jury.[330] The interchange of terminology and concepts may seem like a small thing, but in its effect of blurring the distinctions between the two systems, it sets up a hollow analogy. The reader becomes indignant that military panels are selected contrary to the Constitutional provisions governing civil jury selection. Following these preparatory steps, it is a simple matter to transfer jury

---

[328] *See, e.g.,* Barry, *supra* note 22, at 103 ("In the United States, however, this troublesome issue of the CA as prosecutor remains."); Glazier, *supra* note 22, at 4 ("At best, military jury selection incorporates the varied individual biases of numerous convening authorities and their subordinates. At worst, it involves their affirmative misconduct. 'Court-stacking' is consistently achieved, suspected, or both."); Young, *supra* note 22, at 106 ("Article 25(d)(2) . . . is the problem. . . . As long as the person responsible for sending a case to trial is the same person who selects the court members, the perception of unfairness will not abate.").

[329] For examples of the indiscriminate interchange of terminology, see, for example, Glazier, *supra* note 22, who consistently refers to military juries, and asserts that the panel always has been a jury; Lamb, *supra* note 22, who consistently switches between using the terms "jury" and "panel" to refer to a courts-martial panel; and Rudloff, *supra* note 22, who uses the term "jury" almost exclusively to refer to courts-martial panels. Surprisingly, the military appellate courts occasionally interchange the terms. *See, e.g.,* United States v. Upshaw, 49 M.J. 111, 114 (1998) ("perhaps some of these cases which challenge the convening authority's role and methods in selecting the members of the jury for the trial of appellant will be resolved if Congress passes legislation which will mandate random selection of jury members") (Sullivan, J., concurring); United States v. Ryan, 5 M.J. 97 (C.M.A. 1978) (freely interchanging the terms "jury," and "jurors" with "panel" and "members"). It should also be noted that some commentators seeking to change the system are scrupulous in maintaining the difference in terminology. *See, e.g.,* Young, *supra* note 22 (consistently using the appropriate courts-martial terminology but applying jury selection concepts and principles); McCormack, *supra* note 22 (carefully noting the differences between a military panel and a jury but applying concepts and principles of the jury to the panel selection process).

[330] The analysis of the civilian jury system has attained the status in military legal writing of certain stock characters in popular romances: just as no romance is complete without a tall, dark, handsome and mysterious stranger, few articles on courts-martial reform are complete without an analysis of the development of the civilian jury system. Three of the more recent examples include Glazier, *supra* note 22, at 6-44, who leads off his article with a thorough analysis of the development of the jury system and asserts that courts-martial were unconstitutionally left out of the process; Lamb, *supra* note 22, at 105-113, who begins with a review of jury development from antiquity; and McCormack, *supra* note 22, at 1016-1027, who discusses the history and role of the jury system from ancient Greece to modern times.

goals and jurisprudence to the court-martial system.[331] Various solutions are then proposed, almost all offering a form of random selection coupled with appropriate revisions to UCMJ Article 25.[332] Many commentators are enamored by the promise of computers,[333] which promise to simplify all tasks relating to panel administration and add a disinterested analytical purity to the system.

There are three basic problems with this line of attack. First, in blurring the lines between juries and courts-martial panels, proponents of change either dismiss or fail to take cognizance of the considerable structural barriers between courts-martial panels and petit jury trials. Second, random selection solution offers illusory change that is more form than

---

[331] The transfer of concepts takes several forms. Lamb directly compares the courts-martial process with the ABA standards for jury selection in criminal trials and federal practice, concluding that the military system falls short in many areas. *See* Lamb, *supra* note 22, at 129-132. Glazier takes the more radical approach that the Supreme Court has been wrong for over one hundred and fifty years in interpreting the Sixth Amendment to exclude courts-martial from the jury trial guarantee; he would adopt a random selection system to the military structure and, in his words, exceed the constitutional standards. *See* Glazier, *supra* note 22, at 72-91. McCormack takes a principled look at the goals of the jury system, analogizes those goals to the panel selection process, and suggests random selection. *See* McCormack, *supra* note 22, at 1023-1027, 1048-1050. Young briefly discusses the parameters of the civilian system and spends most of the article focusing on random selection as a method that will eliminate the perceived shortcomings of the system. *See* Young, *supra* note 22, at 93-94, 106-08. The Cox Commission dispenses with analysis altogether in proclaiming that there is no aspect of military criminal procedure that diverges further from civilian practice than the convening authority selecting panel members and recommends random selection from lists provided by the commander. *See* Cox COMMISSION, *supra* note 23, at 7.

[332] *See generally supra* note 22.

[333] Glazier, for example, envisions a "computer-maintained" database for court members, operated by the installation G-1 as an additional duty. Database fields would include name, rank, report date, and availability. In what would surely be a personnel officer's nightmare, the availability field would require constant updating to account for leave, deployments, temporary duty, and so forth. During wartime, the senior in-theater commander would create "virtual installations" that would use this marvelous program to manage courts-martial that might take place in theater. *See* Glazier, *supra* note 22, at 68-72. In a lecture at the Judge Advocate General's School of the Army, David Schlueter advocated random selection as an alternative and says that a computer could be programmed with Article 25 criteria to produce a cross-section of officers and enlisted personnel. He said, "I cannot imagine that the same ingenuity that coordinate the massive air strikes in the Middle East could not be used to select court members for a court-martial when a service member's liberty and property interests are at stake. Schlueter, *supra* note 22, at 20. Young establishes a broad random selection scheme and recommends the use of a computer program to manage it, but provides no details about how the program would work. *See* Young, *supra* note 22, at 118-20.

substance. Third, random selection adds additional complexity to courts-martial administration and interferes with the systemic goals of efficiency, effectiveness, and utility under a wide variety of circumstances.

2. Response: The Structural Barriers and Theoretical Inconsistencies of Applying the Jury-Selection Template to Courts-Martial

a. Article III and the Sixth Amendment as Structural Barriers

In creating a new nation, the Framers had the opportunity to curb the powers of the government, guarantee individual rights and freedoms, and break from the customs and traditions of a system that had oppressed them. Through the Constitution, they were able to remedy the ills caused by a sovereign who "affected to render the Military independent of and superior to the Civil Power,"[334] "made Judges dependent on his Will alone, for the Tenure of their Offices, and the Amount and Payment of their Salaries,"[335] and who "depriv[ed] us, in many Cases, of the Benefits of Trial by Jury."[336] As we have already seen, the Framers ensured that the military would be dependent on and submissive to the civil power by making the President the commander-in-chief[337] but granting the Congress power over the purse.[338] To remedy the lack of judicial independence, the Framers provided tenure

---

[334] THE DECLARATION OF INDEPENDENCE para. 14 (U.S. 1776).

[335] *Id.* para. 11.

[336] *Id.* para. 20.

[337] U.S. CONST. art. II.

[338] *Id.* art. I, § 8, cl. 12.

and salary protections for Article III judges.[339] And to ensure that the right to trial by jury

could not be tampered with, they enshrined it in the basic text of the Constitution.[340]

There can be little doubt that the guarantee of trial by a jury of peers is one of the salutary

civil rights enjoyed by a free people. Blackstone once responded to a critic of the British

Empire who predicted its downfall by observing, "the writer should have recollected that

Rome, Sparta and Carthage, at the time their liberties were lost, were strangers to the trial by

jury."[341] And yet, even as they provided for trial by petit jury both in the text of the

Constitution itself[342] and also in the Bill of Rights,[343] the Framers structurally denied it to

military personnel being tried by courts-martial.

In analyzing the exclusion of courts-martial from the jury trial guarantee, this section will

examine three areas: first, the Framers' first-hand familiarity with military justice; second,

the probable reasons for the inapplicability of the Article III jury trial guarantee to courts-

martial; and third, the Constitutional impossibility of the Sixth Amendment jury trial right

applying to courts-martial.

---

[339] *Id.* art. III, § 1.

[340] Article III of the Constitution states:

> The Trial of all Crimes, except in Cases of Impeachment; shall be by Jury; and such Trial shall be held
> in the State where the said Crimes shall have been committed; but when not committed within any
> State, the Trial shall be at such Place or Places as the Congress may by Law have directed.

Id. art. III, § 2, cl. 3.

[341] 2 WILLIAM BLACKSTONE, COMMENTARIES 379, *quoted in* United States v. Dorr, 195 U.S. 138, 157 (1904)
(Harlan, J., dissenting).

[342] U.S. CONST. art. III, § 2.

[343] *Id.* amend. VI.

One cannot argue that the Framers excluded courts-martial from the Constitutional petit jury trial guarantees out of ignorance. To the contrary, the men who gathered to write the Constitution had considerable military experience and well understood the place of the military in society. They also understood the importance of fundamental civil rights and knew how to balance the demands of civil society with the needs of the military. Eugene Van Loan has written, "[f]amiliarity with the arts and ways of war was . . . a prominent part of the cultural heritage of the architects of the Constitution."[344] Every one of the original colonies had been authorized, either explicitly or implicitly, to form local defense organizations to help combat the hostile environment of the new world.[345] The colonies had enacted universal military training and rudimentary articles of war, and many colonists gained military experience both serving in and leading these militia units.[346] During the French and Indian War from 1754-1763, the British recruited regiments of colonial volunteers that were organized as quasi-regular units and were subject to the British Articles of War; many colonists also served in the British Navy during this time period and were subject to British naval justice.[347]

Thus, by the time the Revolutionary War began, there was already a strong military tradition in the United States. Many of those who were responsible for the Constitution and

---

[344] Van Loan, *supra* note 149, at 379.

[345] *See id.*

[346] *See id.*

[347] *See id.* at 379-80.

the Bill of Rights served in the military during the Revolutionary War.[348] John Marshall, for example, who figured prominently in the Virginia ratification convention and helped draft Virginia's proposals for a federal bill of rights, had been the Army's Deputy Judge Advocate during the war.[349] When the Constitutional Convention convened in 1787, a number of delegates--including George Washington--had served in the Revolutionary War and subsequent Indian wars or had been otherwise involved in the military affairs of the United States.[350]

It is evident that the Framers were intimately familiar with the processes of military justice. They had been subject to it and had used it to help mold the army that beat the British. They recognized its benefits--as John Adams said, the system had carried two empires to the head of civilization[351]--even as they were wary of its potential for excess.[352] One must assume that even if the original decision to incorporate the British Articles of War had been "witless,"[353] the subsequent integration of a separate, legislatively controlled military justice system into both the Articles of Confederation and the Constitution was deliberate and volitional.

---

[348] Henderson, *supra* note 94, at 299.

[349] *Id.*

[350] Van Loan, *supra* note 149, at 387.

[351] *See* Journals, *supra* note 122, at 670-71 n.2.

[352] For example, the Continental Congress declined to apply martial law to the new Northwest Territory to fill the gap until the civil government had established itself. *See* Van Loan, *supra* note 149, at 385.

[353] *See supra* note 125 and accompanying text (comments of Brigadier General Samuel Ansell).

Likewise, excluding the military from the right to trial by jury was a deliberate and volitional act. Trial by jury was one of the few guarantees adopted by the convention in the text of the Constitution itself.[354] There was little debate on this provision,[355] and none at all related to its applicability to courts-martial.[356] Nevertheless, it has always been generally accepted that the provision did not apply to courts-martial.[357] There are several reasons for this assumption, supported by sound logic or authoritative Constitutional jurisprudence.

First, the silence of the Framers concerning courts-martial and the Article III jury trial right speaks volumes. The Framers had already specifically ensured the continuation of an established practice of legislative promulgation of rules for the government of the armed forces.[358] They said nothing about jury trials in connection with courts-martial. On this issue of silence, Eugene Van Loan has elegantly written,

> Neither the words themselves nor the recorded legislative history specifically reveal what relationship, if any, the jury was meant to have to the court-martial. Nevertheless, the documented familiarity of the convention delegates with the nature of each institution may indicate that their silence suggests that

---

[354] U.S. CONST. art. III, § 2; *see also* Van Loan, *supra* note 149, at 395 (discussing the constitutional guarantees adopted by the Convention)

[355] Van Loan, *supra* note 149, at 395.

[356] *Id.*; *see also* Henderson, *supra* note 94, at 300.

[357] *See, e.g.*, Henderson, *supra* note 94, at 300 (observing that it was clear the Framers did not intend the jury trial right to extend to courts-martial). *But see* Glazier, *supra* note 22, at 16 (asserting that because the text of Article III does not exclude courts-martial as it does cases in impeachment, the jury trial right necessarily extends to courts-martial).

[358] *See supra* note 157 and accompanying text.

the jury and the court-martial were contemplated to have no constitutional relationship whatever.[359]

Furthermore, there is a good argument to be made that the Framers intended the Article III jury trial guarantee merely as a codification of a contemporary common law jury trial right that did not extend to trials by court-martial. There is sound jurisprudential support for this point of view. In *Callan v. Wilson*,[360] the Supreme Court stated its conviction that Article III "is to be interpreted in the light of the principles which, at common law, determined whether the accused, in a given class of cases, was entitled to be tried by a jury."[361] At common law, there was no right to a jury trial in a court-martial;[362] the court-martial itself provided its own procedures and system of due process.

The Supreme Court recognized early on that the power to provide for the trial and punishment of servicemembers is "given without any connection between it and the 3d article of the Constitution defining the judicial power of the United States."[363] This does not mean that "courts-martial somehow are not courts, or that [they] somehow decide cases while

---

[359] Van Loan, *supra* note 149, at 396.

[360] 127 U.S. 540 (1888).

[361] *Id.* at 549. The Court expressly found that the common law provided a jury trial for the offense of conspiracy. *Id.*

[362] *See Ex parte* Quirin, 317 U.S. 1, 39 (1942) ("Presentment by a grand jury and trial by a jury of the vicinage where the crime was committed were at the time of the adoption of the Constitution familiar parts of the machinery for criminal trials in the civil courts. But they were procedures unknown to military tribunals."); and Frederick Bernays Wiener, *Courts-Martial and the Bill of Rights: The Original Practice*, 72 HARV. L. REV. 1, 10 (1958) (noting that at the time the Constitution was written, most military offenses were not even cognizable at common law and observing that the jurisdiction of courts-martial has expanded considerably since then).

[363] Dynes v. Hoover, 61 U.S. (20 How.) 65, 79 (1858).

avoiding 'judicial' behavior."[364] Rather, it means that when courts-martial perform judicial functions, they do not partake of "the judicial Power" embodied in Article III.[365] Trial by jury as guaranteed in Article III does not, therefore, structurally exist as a Constitutional right at courts-martial.

Nor does the jury trial guarantee of the Sixth Amendment apply to courts-martial. The Sixth Amendment, like Article III, is unequivocal in its language: "In all criminal prosecutions, the accused shall enjoy the right to a speedy and public trial, by an impartial jury of the State and district wherein the crime shall have been committed."[366] This language does not expressly exclude courts-martial, but as with Article III, the generally accepted view is that it does not apply to courts-martial.[367] Two main factors support this conclusion. First, analysis of the constitutional drafting process indicates that the Framers intended for courts-martial to be excluded from the Sixth Amendment petit jury guarantee. Second, authoritative jurisprudence has forever linked the military exclusion from grand jury presentment under the Fifth Amendment[368] with the petit jury right under the Sixth Amendment.

---

[364] Stern, *supra* note 242, at 1055.

[365] *Id.*

[366] U.S. CONST. amend. VI.

[367] *See, e.g.*, United States v. Smith, 27 M.J. 242 (C.M.A. 1988) (observing that "the right to trial by jury has no application to the appointment of members of courts-martial"). *But see* Glazier, *supra* note 22, at 15 ("The language of the Constitution and the process and history of its drafting support the opposite inference.").

[368] The applicable part of the Fifth Amendment reads thus: "No person shall be held to answer for a capital, or otherwise infamous crime, unless on presentment or indictment of a Grand Jury, except in cases arising in the land or naval forces, or in the Militia, when in actual service in time of War or public danger." U.S. CONST. amend V.

There is little question that in the drafts leading up to the final versions of the Fifth and Sixth Amendments, draftsmen intended to exclude the military both from the right of presentment before a grand jury and trial before a petit jury. Although both of these rights had been a part of the common law for centuries,[369] they never had been a feature of the courts-martial system, which developed independent of the common law. There appeared to be a common understanding among the states that these rights--and particularly the right to trial by petit jury--did not apply at courts-martial.[370] Accordingly, the states that submitted proposed language for a bill of rights to Congress included provisions excepting the military from the jury guarantees.[371]

The Fifth and Sixth Amendments had a common ancestor in the amendments that were adopted by the House and sent to the Senate for confirmation. Article the Tenth, as the House proposal was denominated, read thus:

> Tenth. The trial of all crimes (except in cases of impeachment, and in cases arising in the land and naval forces, or in the militia when in actual service in time of war or public danger) shall be by an impartial Jury of the vicinage, with the requisite of unanimity for conviction, the right of challenge, and other accustomed requisites; and no person shall be held to answer for a capital, or otherways [*sic*] crime, unless on a presentment or indictment by a Grand Jury;

---

[369] *See* Wiener, *supra* note 362, at 3.

[370] *See generally* Henderson, *supra* note 94, at 305-309. In this section, Henderson reviews the provisions of several states' bills of rights pertaining to jury trials and the military. He notes that even in states that did not expressly except the military from these guarantees (Maryland, North Carolina, Pennsylvania, Vermont, and Virginia), the states used courts-martial to govern their militia, "to which the jury trial guarantees were clearly not meant to apply." *Id.* at 306.

[371] *See generally*, *id.* at 306-310. Interestingly, some of the same states that failed expressly to exclude the military from their own Bill of Rights did so in the proposals they submitted to Congress. For example, Virginia, Maryland, and North Carolina all included similar provisions excluding the military from the jury trial guarantees. *Id.*

but if a crime be committed in a place in possession of an enemy, or in which an insurrection may prevail, the indictment and trial may by law be authorized in some other place within the State.[372]

The Senate objected to the House version. Initially, the Senate stripped the House's Tenth Article of its petit jury guarantee and, a few days later, combined the grand jury provision (including the military exclusion) with another proposed amendment concerning double jeopardy and due process of law. This proposed amendment became our present Fifth Amendment.[373]

The Senate action stemmed from disagreements between the two legislative bodies concerning the nature and extent of the vicinage[374] from which the jury was to be drawn. The Senate was initially willing to discard the jury trial guaranty rather than yield on the issue of vicinage.[375] Significantly, there is no evidence that the Senate's dispute with the House's article had anything to do with excluding the military from the petit jury guarantee.[376]

Eventually, the two houses reached a compromise on the vicinage issue that guaranteed the jury would be at least drawn from the same state in which the crime was committed, but

---

[372] Henderson, *supra* note 94, at 312 (quoting S. JOUR., 1ST CONG., 1ST SESS. 114-19, 121-27, 129-31 (1789)).

[373] *Id.* at 412-13.

[374] The word "vicinage" means "vicinity" or "proximity" and is used to indicate "the locale from which the accused is entitled to have the jurors selected." *See* BLACK'S LAW DICTIONARY 1561 (7th ed. 1999).

[375] *See* Van Loan, *supra* note 149, at 409.

[376] *See* Henderson, *supra* note 94, at 313.

giving Congress the authority to define the vicinage later through the creation of judicial districts.[377] The petit jury guarantee, however, was never recombined with the grand jury guarantee. Instead, it was placed with the Senate's Eighth Article after the guarantee of a speedy and public trial, and the military exclusion language was not duplicated; this amendment became our present Sixth Amendment.[378] Thus, what started out as one common amendment was split into two by virtue of a disagreement that had nothing to do with military justice.

There is nothing in the record to indicate why the Senate did not simply recombine the compromise petit jury guarantee with the original grand jury language, thereby ensuring that the military exclusion would explicitly have applied to them both. The most likely possibility, according to Henderson and Van Loan, was that it was an oversight due to the exhaustion of the members of Congress.[379] This theory makes sense when one considers the timing involved in the passage of the amendments. The Congress could not adjourn until the amendments were passed, and when the conference committee was appointed on September 21, 1789, the members of Congress were already tired and were eager to return home.[380] The

---

[377] Van Loan, *supra* note 149, at 409.

[378] *Id.*

[379] *See* Van Loan, *supra* note 149, at 411-412; Henderson, *supra* note 94, at 305, 323.

[380] *See* Van Loan, *supra* note 149, at 411.

committee met in haste, finishing its work September 24; by September 29 the amendments had passed both houses and Congress was adjourned.[381]

However, we are not left simply with speculation on the matter. Further evidence of contemporary Congressional intent is provided by an act reported to the House on 17 September 1789, "to recognise, and adapt to the Constitution of the United States, the establishment of the troops raised under the resolves of the United States in Congress assembled."[382] Section 4 of the act prescribed that the army would be governed by the rules and articles of war established by Congress, a "manifestation of Congress's recognition-- during the very period in which it passed the Bill of Rights--that the army was to be continued to be governed by its traditional and separate system of courts-martial, unaffected by the proposed new amendment guaranteeing the right to trial by petit jury."[383]

In addition to the evidence of Congressional intent from the drafting process and contemporary legislation, the Supreme Court has also provided authoritative jurisprudence on the exclusion of courts-martial from the Sixth Amendment jury trial guarantee. In *Ex Parte Milligan*,[384] the Court addressed the issue of whether Lamdin P. Milligan, a U.S. citizen, had been properly tried by a military commission in Indiana during the civil war. The Court held that the trial violated Milligan's rights by subjecting him to a non-Article III

---

[381] *See id.*

[382] *See id.* at 413.

[383] *Id.* at 414.

[384] 71 U.S. 2 (1866).

tribunal and denying him the right to presentment by grand jury and trial before a petit jury

during a time when the Federal authority in Indiana was unopposed and the courts were

open.[385] In analyzing the case, the Court made a statement in dicta that has, over the years,

evolved in to the force of a holding, "the framers of the Constitution, doubtless, meant to

limit the right of trial by jury, in the sixth amendment, to those persons who were subject to

indictment or presentment in the fifth."[386] This linkage has been consistently interpreted, not

only by the Supreme Court, but also the military appellate courts, to preclude courts-martial

from the Sixth Amendment jury trial guarantee.[387]

There have been efforts to demonstrate that the Supreme Court's refusal to apply the

Article III or sixth amendment jury trial guarantees to courts-martial is wrong or even

unconstitutional.[388] However, the fact is that in the structure and framework of the

Constitution and its amendments, the Framers forever barred trial by jury at courts-martial as

a matter of right. Inasmuch as Congress has not chosen to statutorily grant a jury trial at

---

[385] *Id.* at 121-23.

[386] *Id.* at 123.

[387] *See, e.g.*, Whelchel v. McDonald, 340 U.S. 122, 127 (1950) ("The right to trial by jury guaranteed by the Sixth Amendment is not applicable to trials by courts-martial or military commissions. Courts-martial have been composed of officers both before and after the adoption of the Constitution."); *Ex parte* Quirin, 317 U.S. 1, 40 (1942) ("'cases arising in the land or naval forces' are deemed excepted by implication from the Sixth Amendment."); United States v. Smith, 27 M.J. 242, 248 (C.M.A. 1988) ("The right of trial by jury has no application to the appointment of members of courts-martial.").

[388] *See, e.g.*, Glazier, *supra* note 22, at 8-22 (asserting that it the Supreme Court's failure to apply the Article III and sixth amendment jury guarantees to courts-martial is an old and flawed judicial creation); Remcho, *supra* note 22, at 204 (claiming that there is "questionable precedential support" for the Supreme Court's analysis that Article III and the Sixth Amendment jury trial guarantees do not apply to courts-martial). *But see* O'Connor, *supra* note 285, at n.76 ("Although the author agrees that the Court's statements in Milligan regarding servicemembers' Sixth Amendment jury right are technically dicta, the author simply cannot accept Major Glazier's ably-presented argument that the centuries-old practice of conducting courts-martial without a jury of the accused's peers somehow now runs afoul of the Constitution.").

courts-martial, it is a mistake to carelessly mingle the jurisprudence of Sixth Amendment

jury selection with the Constitutionally and functionally different process of court-martial

panel member selection.

b. Random Selection and the Illusion of Form Over Substance

Attempts to reform the panel member selection process through random selection elevate

form over substance. This is largely because the consequences of a pure random selection

system are virtually inconceivable in a military setting. The majority of service members are

in the junior enlisted ranks, young, and with relatively little military experience.[389] In a pure

random selection scheme--one that would actually embody the Supreme Court[390] and ABA[391]

ideal of a randomly selected cross-section of the community--these junior members would

most likely comprise a substantial percentage of any given court-martial panel. To be a

purist--to meet the ideal--one would have to be willing to discard a number of venerable and

practical military justice customs: the tradition that one's actions will never be judged by

someone junior in rank or experience,[392] the philosophy that those who judge will be

sufficiently acquainted with the principles of good order and discipline to place alleged

---

[389] According to a recent statistical report, approximately 62.5% of all servicemembers in the Department of Defense are in the ranks E-5 and below. 46.8% of all active duty personnel are 25 years old or younger. *See* MILITARY FAMILY RESOURCE CTR., U.S. DEP'T OF DEFENSE, PROFILE OF THE MILITARY COMMUNITY: 2001 DEMOGRAPHICS REPORT (2001), *available at* http://www.mfrc.calib.com/stat.cfm.

[390] *See* Williams v. Florida, 399 U.S. 78, 100 (1970) (stating that a jury drawn from a representative cross section of the community is an essential element of due process).

[391] *See* ABA STANDARDS *supra* note 323, Standard 15.2.1(a) ("The names of those persons who may be called for jury service should be selected at random from sources which will furnish a representative cross-section of the community.").

[392] This tradition is embodied in UCMJ art. 25(d)(1) (2002) ("When it can be avoided, no member of an armed force may be tried by a court-martial any member of which is junior to him in rank or grade.").

offenses in their proper context,[393] the statutory mandate to assure that those who serve on courts-martial are "best-qualified" for the duty.[394]

Few are willing to abandon those unique benefits or essential characteristics of the military justice system. And so reformers propose modifications of random selection. Let the commander choose a list of those whom he believes to be qualified, and randomly select from that list.[395] Screen individuals for Article 25(d)(2) criteria, and then spit out a randomly generated list.[396] Appoint an independent jury commissioner to make the selections.[397] Presumptively disqualify a major percentage of service members--those below the grade of E-3, for example--and randomly select from the rest.[398] Modify the Article 25(d)(2) criteria to make them more easily fit a computer database model and facilitate random selection.[399] Modify the random selection criteria to ensure that all panel members are senior to the

---

[393] This hearkens back to the earliest days of military justice tribunals. For example, under the Gustavus Adolphus Code, the membership of the higher court-martial included the top leadership of the army, every regimental colonel, and even colonels from other nations. *See supra* note 62 and accompanying text.

[394] UCMJ art. 25(d)(2) (2002).

[395] COX COMMISSION, *supra* note 23, at 7.

[396] *See, e.g.*, Brookshire, *supra* note 22, at 100-02 (establishing screening criteria to be used prior to random selection).

[397] *See, e.g.*, Lamb, *supra* note 22, at 161-62.

[398] *See, e.g.*, Hodson, *supra* note 22, at 64 (suggesting that E-1 through E-3 should probably be presumptively disqualified); Young, *supra* note 22, at 119 (suggesting that all service members, officer and enlisted, with less than two years' military service be excluded). A modified version of this approach already has been sanctioned by the Court of Military Appeals as consistent with UCMJ art. 25(d)(2), provided that the convening authority personally approves the results of the random selection. *See infra* notes 406-411 and accompanying text.

[399] *See, e.g.*, Glazier, *supra* note 22, at 68 (recommending that art. 25 be abandoned); Lamb, *supra* note 22, at 160 (recommending that the subjective criteria of art. 25 be abandoned); Young, *supra* note 22, at Appendix (deleting subjective criteria of art. 25 from proposed revision of art. 25); McCormack, *supra* 22, at Appendix (deleting subjective criteria of art. 25 from proposed revision).

accused and that the "random selection" produces a cross-section of rank. [400] Do anything, in short, but accept the consequences of an actual random selection scheme.

In building the illusion that random selection solves the perceived problems of panel member selection, reformers tend to ignore or downplay the inconvenient theoretical inconsistencies of their proposals. It is almost as if random selection is its own goal, no matter how removed the proposed modifications might take it from the justifications that were used to claim its necessity. Moreover, no one addresses how random selection would change anything but a perception; those commanders who truly desire to unlawfully influence courts-martial will find a way to do it regardless of the personnel or methods involved in panel member selection.[401] As the Joint Service Committee concluded, "even a completely random method of selection may not improve perceptions of command influence because members will still be subject to the orders, assignments, and evaluations of the

---

[400] *See, e.g.*, Glazier, *supra* note 22, at 101-103 (maintaining the seniority requirement of art. 25(d)(1) and proposing rank-group restrictions on pure randomness to obtain a better cross-section); *see also* Young, *supra* note 22, at 120-21 (recommending that because military demographics are so weighted toward the young and inexperienced, the random selection program should guarantee a cross-section of the military by grade).

[401] *See* Spak & Thomes, *supra* note 22, at 535:

> Similarly, revamping the court-member selection process and renewing emphasis on the prohibition against retaliatory action against court members would not change the fact that commanders can easily harm the careers of court members by taking actions that stop short of violating Article 37(b). And court members know it. A poor convening authority can give a court member a bad efficiency report for his or her part in reaching a decision that the convening authority dislikes. A more savvy one would "damn with faint praise."

Id.

superiors who refer charges to trial."[402] In essence, reformers have cried out, "The Emperor is naked!" and then suggested clothing him with fig leaves and pasties.

c. Mandatory Random Selection Undermines the Unique Goals of the Military Justice System

Mandatory random selection, in removing the commander from the panel selection process, sends the message that the military justice system is more important than the military. At best, random selection confers no actual benefit on the military justice system. At worst, it adds additional administrative burdens that needlessly complicate the system, reduce its efficiency, and most critically, withdraw from commanders the ability to direct the disposition of their personnel. Random selection destroys the discretion of convening authorities to select specialized panels based on the unique needs of a case.[403] In addition, random selection deprives the accused of the important benefit of knowing in advance the names and dispositions of those who will judge him, thus permitting him to intelligently decide whether it will be in his best interests to select trial before a panel or before a military

---

[402] JSC REPORT, *supra* note 29.

[403] Under the current system, a convening authority is free to select panel members who have specialized knowledge or experience. *See, e.g.*, United States v. Lynch, 35 M.J. 579 (C.G.C.M.R. 1992). In *Lynch*, the accused was a commander who was tried for hazarding a vessel when his Coast Guard buoy tender ran aground. The general court-martial convening authority selected a panel in which all members had experience as commanders afloat. The accused complained of panel-stacking, but the Coast Guard court disagreed, holding that such a court, by virtue of its training and experience, would better be able to understand the evidence and apply it to the standard of care expected of a commanding officer. *Id.* at 587. *See also* United States v. Simpson, 55 M.J. 674, 691-92 (A.C.C.A. 2001) (upholding a convening authority's decision to exclude all members from the accused's unit from a panel in order to keep the panel free from individuals who might have been tainted by prior exposure to the investigation, the accused, the victims, and witnesses); United States v. Brocks, 55 M.J. 614, 616 (A.F.C.C.A. 2001), *aff'd*, 2002 CAAF LEXIS 1614 (2002) (upholding a convening authority's decision to exclude members of the Base Medical Group from a court-martial panel in order to have a fair trial because all four conspirators and many of the witnesses came from that group).

judge sitting alone.[404] Many mandatory random selection schemes would deprive the accused of his ability to choose between an officer and mixed officer-and-enlisted panel.[405]

However, if a convening authority chooses to use random selection in order to assist in narrowing the field of candidates from whom she will personally select a court-martial panel, that option is already available. The great, untold secret of random selection is that it has been legally available as a method of panel member selection for nearly a quarter-century.

In *United States v. Yager*,[406] the accused was tried before a panel that had been randomly selected pursuant to a local regulation at Fort Riley, Kansas.[407] The random selection program at Fort Riley was designed to dovetail with the requirements of UCMJ Article 25(d)(2). The installation used personnel data files and screening questionnaires to create a list of qualified panel members, from whose ranks the courts-martial panels were randomly selected prior to final approval by the general court-martial convening authority.[408] The accused appealed on the basis that rank had impermissibly been used as a criteria to systematically exclude low-ranking personnel. The Court of Military Appeals affirmed the conviction, holding that the exclusion of E-1s and E-2s was in accordance with the statutory

---

[404] *Cf.* Young, *supra* note 22, at 117 (dismissing the importance of the ability to assess whether a known panel or judge will be more lenient).

[405] UCMJ art. 25(c)(1) permits an accused to select a panel consisting of at least one-third enlisted membership. The presumption is that if he does not make that request, the panel will consist of officers only. *See* UCMJ art. 25(c)(1) (2002). The random selection schemes proposed by Lamb and Young recommend eliminating this choice. *See* Lamb, *supra* note 22, at 160-61; Young, *supra* note 22, at 108.

[406] 7 M.J. 171 (C.M.A. 1979).

[407] *Id.*

[408] *Id.*

criteria of Article 25(d)(2), because application of the criteria would have excluded most of them anyway.[409] The CMA also approved of the random selection method, provided that the convening authority made the final decision based on Article 25(d)(2) criteria.[410]

Yager did not initiate a stampede to try random selection, despite later CMA opinions intimating that random selection coupled with convening authority approval of the final panel would not run afoul of UCMJ Article 25(d)(2).[411] Instead, Yager has been an anomaly of panel-selection jurisprudence.

Naturally enough, this leads to the question, why hasn't random selection been more popular in the military? In answering this question, it is worth taking a closer look at the system employed in Yager. The system, as already noted, was not pure random selection; the lower two enlisted ranks were presumptively disqualified, as were soldiers who were not U.S. citizens.[412] Moreover, the convening authority had directed that each court-martial panel would contain at least two field grade officers, each special court-martial would contain at least three officers, and each general court-martial panel would include at least four officers.[413] In order to obtain qualified panels, the installation staff judge advocate sent

---

[409] Id. at 173.

[410] Id. at 171.

[411] See United States v. Smith, 27 M.J. 242, 249 (C.M.A. 1988).

[412] Yager, 7 M.J. at 171. The CMA did not address the issue of exclusion of citizens for two reasons: it was not raised at the trial level, and the accused was himself a U.S. citizen. Id. at 173.

[413] See JSC REPORT, supra note 29, app. J, at 3.

detailed questionnaires to prospective court members.[414] Those who did not return the

questionnaires--and over one-quarter of the soldiers did not--were presumptively

disqualified.[415] Once the questionnaires arrived at the staff judge advocate's office, they had

to be screened in order to create a qualified panel.[416] The administrative burden for both the

SJA and the installation personnel office was enormous. A computer system would do little

to speed up the process of mailing, tracking, opening, or entering data from questionnaires.

The results of the experiment were, in addition, somewhat unclear. Not many cases were

actually tried before panels,[417] and the military judge at Fort Riley felt that the panels failed

to meet the "best qualified" criteria. The judge noted, somewhat acerbically, "[s]o far as I

know, no one has ever contended that jurors should be immature, uneducated, inexperienced,

have no familiarity with the military service, and have no judicial temperament."[418] He also

criticized the program because, in order to comply with the law, the convening authority still

---

[414] *Id.*

[415] *Id.* This process, in itself, would create interesting panel selection issues. In essence, panel members were permitted to self-select themselves either on or off the panel, depending on whether they completed the questionnaire. Thus, panels could potentially be skewed toward soldiers with an interest in military justice, soldiers with an agenda who hoped to serve on panels, and soldiers and officers with non-demanding jobs who felt they had enough leisure time to serve on courts. In contrast, some of the best-qualified potential panel members may have escaped consideration for service simply by failing to turn in the questionnaire.

[416] *Id.*

[417] *Id.* at 4.

[418] *See* Letter from Colonel Robert L. Wood, Military Judge, to Major Rex Brookshire, Deputy Staff Judge Advocate, Fort Riley, Kansas (Dec. 13, 1974), at 6, *reprinted in* JSC REPORT, *supra* note 402, app. K.

had to personally appoint the panel; all the program accomplished was to force him to select those who were not, in his opinion, necessarily the best qualified.[419]

There are several lessons to be learned from this experience. First, a pure random selection system did not meet the needs of Article 25(d)(2) or the convening authority. The convening authority had to force a cross-section of ranks by mandating minimum numbers of officers and field-grade officers on the panel. Second, the questionnaire method of determining qualifications permitted soldiers to self-select their participation in courts-martial panels. Some of the best-qualified officers and soldiers on the installation may have declined to fill in a questionnaire, considering themselves too busy with other duties. Third, the system created an enormous administrative burden on the personnel office and staff judge advocate's office at the installation. Fourth, and perhaps most important, the quality of the panels was degraded.

When rhetoric and inapposite comparisons with the jury system are replaced by examination of the actual effects random selection would have on the military, reason demonstrates that the current system best balances the varied needs of the individual services while still producing fair, impartial panels that meet the criteria of UCMJ Article 25(d)(2). Indeed, the JSC, at the direction of Congress, recently concluded as much in a detailed study of the effects random selection might have on the military.[420] Operating under the mandate that a random selection system would still have to produce "best-qualified" members

---

[419] *Id.*

[420] *See* JSC REPORT, *supra* note 29, at 47.

93

according to the criteria of UCMJ Article 25(d)(2), they examined six different alternatives: maintaining the current practice, random nomination of panel members, random selection of panel members, a combination of random nomination and selection, expanding the source of potential panel members, and creating an independent selection authority.[421]

In concluding that the current system best meets the needs of the military, the JSC did not simply "pencil-whip" its analysis to meet pre-conceived conclusions. The committee's report is an honest, thorough, and balanced look at each of the alternatives in light of theory, actual practice, and workability. In view of the varied mission-related needs of the services, including the duty to engage in combat if called upon to do so, the JSC reached some conclusions that ought to give pause to reformers who apparently believe military needs should have no bearing on the military justice system. A selection system must possess certain characteristics in order to be useful in a military setting. It must be "sufficiently flexible to be applied in all units, locations, and operational conditions and across all armed forces."[422] It must recognize that competency and availability decisions are "critical command functions."[423] Random methods do not meet those ends because they are not uniformly operable in all units, locations and conditions and would "present substantial difficulties during heightened military operations to include war or contingency operations."[424] A mandatory random selection scheme would increase administrative

---

[421] *Id.* at 16.

[422] *Id.* at 46.

[423] *Id.*

[424] *Id.*

burdens, lower the overall level of competency of panels, and produce increased delays in the system.[425] In short, mandatory random selection falls far short of its theoretical promise and could actually frustrate the unique goals of the military justice system.

B. Keeping Up with the Joneses: Reform Based on British and Canadian Jurisprudence

1. The Strategy: Argue that American System Must Change to Keep Pace with Court-Mandated Overhaul of British and Canadian Systems

It has become fashionable to disparage the UCMJ in comparison with recent reforms in the British and Canadian systems that significantly modified the role of the court-martial convening authority. The Cox Commission, for example, claimed, "military justice in the United States has stagnated" in comparison with other countries around the world, particularly Great Britain and Canada.[426] The Bar Association for the District of Columbia, in its submission to the Cox Commission, argued that the decisions invalidating the role of the convening authority in Great Britain and Canada are particularly significant because "[t]he Uniform Code of Military Justice . . . shares a common ancestry with the British system found insufficiently independent in *Findlay* and *Lane*. The Canadian system invalidated in *Genereux* shares that common ancestor as well."[427] Guy Glazier writes, "Canada, Great Britain, and the European Community all agree that member selection by the

---

[425] *Id.* at 45.

[426] COX COMMISSION, *supra* note 23, at 3.

[427] Memorandum from the Bar Association of the District of Columbia, to the Cox Commission, subject: Special Considerations Related to the 'Final List of Topics'" 11 (March 13, 2001), *reprinted in*, COX COMMISSION, *supra* note 23, app. C.

convening authority fails to meet minimum standards of independence and impartiality in practice and appearance" and calls it ironic that the United States, which fought for freedom from Great Britain, is alone in the free world in denying trial by jury to service members.[428]

At first blush, these are persuasive arguments. If the country that created the Articles of War saw fit to abandon the practice of convening authority panel selection, why hasn't the United States? If our closest neighbor has rejected the practice, why don't we? Surely our system should meet their minimum standards of independence and impartiality. We must be remarkably obtuse if we have not seen the light and spontaneously changed our military justice system to meet the requirements imposed on Great Britain and Canada by, respectively, the European Court of Human Rights and the Canadian Supreme Court.

There is a certain specious charm to these arguments. However, in measuring the significance of the British and Canadian actions, it is not enough to make the simplistic argument that they have changed and so should we. The decisions must be placed in their proper contextual framework. Furthermore, the practical effect of the changes bears examination as well. As will be seen, the British and Canadian changes were appropriate within a contextual and structural framework that has little, if any, actual relevance to the United States system.

---

[428] Glazier, *supra* note 22, at 88. Glazier's statement about trial by jury is not quite accurate. The British system removed the convening authority from panel selection, but it did not appreciably change trial procedure. Now a Court Martial Administration Officer (CMAO) handpicks the panel based on a list provided by the convening authority. Whatever benefits to freedom and independence this procedure may have, it is not a jury trial.

2. Response: A Structural and Contextual Analysis of the British and Canadian Changes

a. The British System and the European Convention for the Protection of Fundamental Rights and Human Freedoms

In 1951, Great Britain ratified the European Convention for the Protection of Human Rights and Fundamental Freedoms.[429] Most European countries that adopted the Convention had to formally incorporate it into their domestic law under their individual constitutions. In Great Britain, however, the thought was that the rights and freedoms guaranteed by the Convention could be delivered under British common law.[430] As the jurisprudence of the European Court of Human Rights developed, however, it became apparent that British common law was no longer sufficient to vindicate rights under the Convention and incorporation would be necessary.[431] Accordingly, the United Kingdom formally incorporated the Convention into its domestic law in the year 2000.[432]

In the meantime, British citizens who felt the government was violating their human rights under the Convention had recourse to the European Commission of Human Rights and

---

[429] The Council of Europe's Treaty Office maintains an on-line table that lists the dates of signature, ratification, and entry into force of the European Convention for the Protection of Human Rights and Fundamental Freedoms for all member states of the Council of Europe. It is available at http://conventions.coe.int/Treaty/EN/CadreListeTraites.htm.

[430] *See* HUMAN RIGHTS OFFICE, UNITED KINGDOM SEC'Y OF STATE FOR THE HOME DEP'T, WHITE PAPER: RIGHTS BROUGHT HOME: THE HUMAN RIGHTS BILL (1997) [hereinafter WHITE PAPER], *available at* http://www.archive.official-documents.co.uk.

[431] *Id.*

[432] *See* Wing Commander Simon P. Rowlinson, *The British System of Military Justice*, 52 AIR FORCE L. REV. 17, 20 (2002).

the European Court of Human Rights.[433] Under the Convention, the Court of Human Rights

is empowered to award money damages and declare that there has been a violation. In turn,

the signatory nations are obligated to rectify any noted violations in their internal laws.[434]

Article Six of the Convention provides, "In the determination of his civil rights and

obligations or of any criminal charge against him, everyone is entitled to a fair and public

hearing within a reasonable time by an independent and impartial tribunal established by

law."[435] The celebrated case of *Findlay v. United Kingdom*[436] arose under this provision of

the Convention. In 1991, Lance Sergeant Findlay pled guilty to charges of assault, conduct

to the prejudice of good order and discipline, and threatening to kill.[437] He was sentenced by

a court-martial to two years' confinement, reduction in rank, and dismissal.[438] His appeals

through British military channels were denied, and in 1993, he filed a petition with the

European Commission of Human Rights alleging that court-martial procedures under the

Army Act 1955 and implementing regulations deprived him of an independent and impartial

---

[433] WHITE PAPER, *supra* note 430.

[434] *Id.*

[435] European Convention on Human Rights and Fundamental Freedoms, Nov. 4, 1950, art. 6, § 1, ETS No. 5 [hereinafter Convention], *available at* http://www.pfc.org.uk/legal/echrtext.htm.

[436] 24 E.H.R.R. 221 (1997).

[437] *Id.* at paras. 6-10.

[438] *Id.* at para. 23.

tribunal under Article 6(1) of the Convention. The Commission referred the case to the European Court of Human Rights.[439]

The Court found a violation of Article 6(1). In analyzing the independence of the court-martial, the Court looked to the manner of appointment of its members, their term of office, the existence of guarantees against outside pressure, and whether the body presented the appearance of impartiality.[440] The test for impartiality employed a two-pronged analysis in which the court examined whether the tribunal was subjectively biased and whether it was impartial from an objective viewpoint. The court specifically stated that appearances were important in determining independence and impartiality.[441] Because the convening authority was superior in rank to all members of the panel and also acted as the confirming officer in reviewing the sentence, the Court found that the guarantees of independence and impartiality were not satisfied.[442] It is worth noting that the United Kingdom had already legislatively changed its courts-martial system by the time this case went to court.[443]

One wonders if *Findlay* would ever have made it to the Court of Human Rights had the British military justice system contained meaningful appellate rights. In an address at the U.S. Army Judge Advocate General's School, the Judge Advocate General of the Armed

---

[439] *Id.* at paras. 26-28, 58.

[440] *Id.* at para. 73.

[441] *Id.*

[442] *Id.* at paras. 76-80.

[443] *Id.* at paras. 66-67.

Forces of the United Kingdom commented that the European Commission, which certified the case to the Court of Human Rights, might have taken a different view had "the service member been permitted full rights of appeal to a higher civilian court."[444] The review system at the time had the following characteristics: no appeal to a judicial body if the accused pled guilty (as was the case in *Findlay*), the system of confirmation and reviews did not involve consideration by a legal body, the reviews were done in secret, the appellant could not participate in the reviews in any way, and there were no reasons given for denial of relief.[445]

Findlay did cause a change in British military justice. The convening authority no longer plays a role in the system. His former duties have been spread to three different bodies: a Prosecuting Authority, who determines whether to prosecute; a Court-Martial Administration Officer (CMAO), who sets the date and venue for the court-martial and personally selects the members using lists provided by various commanding officers; and Reviewing Officers, who now provide reasons for their decisions.[446] These changes have not ended controversy with the British system, but rather seem to have opened a Pandora's box in which judicial challenges to the legitimacy of the system are the order of the day.[447] In addition, the British

---

[444] Rant, *The British Courts-Martial System: It Ain't Broke, But it Needs Fixing*, 152 MIL. L. REV. 179, 183 (1996)

[445] Ann Lyon, *After Findlay: A Consideration of Some Aspects of the Military Justice System*, 1998 CRIM. L. REV. 109, 113. For an interesting comparison of rights under the UCMJ with the rights Findlay had under the British system, see Lieutenant Colonel Theodore Essex & Major Leslea Tate Pickle, *A Reply to the Report of the Commission on the 50th Anniversary of the Uniform Code of Military Justice (May 2001)--"The Cox Commission"*, 52 AIR FORCE L. REV. 233, 266 (2002). The authors have created a table that provides a side-by-side comparison of the British and UCMJ systems. The UCMJ contains a number of statutory safeguards that ensure independence and impartiality, none of which were available in the British system. *See generally id.*

[446] Lyon, *supra* note 445, at 115-17.

[447] *See, e.g.*, Rowlinson, *supra* note 432, at 43 ("Indeed, it is accurate to say that the number of challenges to the reformed system have been greater in number than those to the system which existed prior to the reforms.").

military has experienced difficulty coping with the increased administrative burdens of the system and has had to adopt a centralized system for trying cases.[448] The British system tries about three hundred courts-martial per year compared to over 4,500 in the American system.[449]

b. *The Canadian System and the Canadian Charter of Rights and Freedoms*

Canada's military justice system, like the United States system, had its roots in the British Articles of War.[450] Until the adoption of the Militia Act of 1868, which organized the Canadian Army,[451] the British Army operated in Canada. The Militia Act, in essence, adopted the British Articles of War. The British military justice system had both a direct and indirect effect on Canadian military justice through World War II; a situation that created a "confusion of authorities" that was remedied with the 1950 National Defense Act (NDA).[452]

Rowlinson notes that many advocates are now attacking the changes as cosmetic only and failed to address the root causes of unfairness and bias in the system. *Id.* With respect to the particular issue of member selection, see John Mackenzie, *Who Really Runs the Court-Martial System*, 150 NEW L.J. 608 (2000). Mr. Mackenzie claims that the CMAO does not truly have the discretion to select court-martial members because he merely nominates the list provided to him by the chain of command.

[448] *See* JSC REPORT, *supra* note 402, app M, at 7.

[449] JSC REPORT, *supra* note 29, at 43.

[450] Brigadier-General Jerry S.T. Pitzul and Commander John C. Maguire, *A Perspective on Canada's Code of Service Discipline*, 52 AIR FORCE L. REV. 1 (2002).

[451] *Id.* at 3.

[452] *Id.* at 4-5.

The NDA created a unified Code of Service Discipline for Canada's different services. This Code continued in force, although it was modified from time to time.[453]

In 1982, Canada experienced a significant change in its domestic law with the adoption of the Canadian Charter of Rights and Freedoms.[454] Article 11(d) of the Charter guarantees that a person charged with an offense has the right "to be presumed innocent until proven guilty according to law in a fair and public hearing by an independent and impartial tribunal."[455] The language is remarkably similar to that in the European Convention on Human Rights and Fundamental Freedoms, and as will be seen, the Canadian Supreme Court has adopted an analysis similar to the one later used by the European Court of Human Rights in *Findlay*.

The seminal case that changed the Canadian military justice system was *R. v. Genereux*,[456] a 1992 case in which a corporal in the Canadian armed forces appealed his general court-martial conviction for drug trafficking and desertion. The main ground for appeal was that a military tribunal did not constitute an independent and impartial tribunal within the meaning of section 11(d) of the Charter.[457]

---

[453] *Id*. at 7-8.

[454] Canadian Charter of Rights and Freedoms, Part I of the Constitution Act, 1982, being Schedule B to the Canada Act 1982 (U.K.), c. 11 (LEXIS 2002) [hereinafter Canadian Charter].

[455] *Id*. at § 11(d).

[456] 1 S.C.R. 259 (1992).

[457] *Id*.

The Supreme Court of Canada took a broad look at the Canadian military justice system in concluding that it violated the Canadian Charter. The guarantees of independence and impartiality were, as in *Findlay*, analyzed not according to actual bias, but according to an objective standard that measured whether a reasonable person would perceive the tribunal as independent.[458] There were three factors required for judicial independence: security of tenure, financial independence, and institutional independence.[459] The Court found that the Canadian general court-martial of the day violated the Charter in several respects.[460] The Court also found that certain aspects of the court-martial could cast into doubt the institutional independence of the proceedings, in particular, the role of the convening authority, who decided when a court-martial would take place, appointed the members of the court, and appointed the prosecutor.[461]

As a result of this opinion, Canada implemented a number of legislative changes to its system of military justice. The convening authority no longer has the authority to appoint judges and panel members.[462] The prosecution function has been centralized and assigned

---

[458] *Id.* at 286.

[459] *Id.* at 301.

[460] Most of the factors are not directly relevant to this paper. The Court found that the structural position of the Judge Advocate General as an agent of the executive was troubling. He had the power to appoint military judges. Their security of tenure was affected by the ad hoc nature of the tribunal and the fact that their promotions, and hence, financial security, could be dependent on good performance evaluations. "A reasonable person could well have entertained the apprehension that the person chosen as judge advocate had been selected because he or she had satisfied the interests of the executive." *See id.* at 303-05. Financial security was an issue both for the judge and the members of the court. At the time, there were no formal prohibitions against evaluating an officer on the basis of his or her performance at court-martial. This could potentially result in negative evaluations, and hence, lower promotion opportunities. *See id.* at 305-06.

[461] *Id.* at 308-09.

[462] Pitzul and McGuire, *supra* note 450, at 8.

exclusively to the Director of Military Prosecutions.[463] Canada has adopted a modified

random selection methodology for appointing court members based on rank, and panels are

appointed centrally under the direction of the Chief Military Trial Judge.[464] All officers

meeting the rank criteria in the Canadian Armed forces with the exception of chaplains, legal

officers, security officers, officers from the accused's unit, and witnesses, are eligible to

serve.[465]

The very first use of the system demonstrated the potential difficulties of a centralized

selection system when the computer selected the military attaché in Malaysia as the President

of a General Court-Martial in eastern Canada.[466] Centralized selection could hamstring the

much larger United States system. The Canadian system does not deal with nearly the

volume of the United States system; only twenty general courts-martial were convened

between 1994 and 1998.[467]

    c. (In)Applicability of the British and Canadian Models to the US Constitutional Framework

The changes to the British and Canadian systems have little bearing on military justice in

the United States. Both countries modified their military justice systems only after making

---

[463] *Id.* at 12.

[464] JSC REPORT, *supra* note 402, app. M, at 2.

[465] *Id.*

[466] *Id.* at 3.

[467] *Id.* at 1.

major changes in their domestic charters governing human rights and freedoms. Neither country changed its military justice system spontaneously; both countries waited until legal challenges made it clear their military justice systems did not meet the new charter obligations as interpreted by applicable jurisprudence.

Although the common ancestry of the three systems is the same, the United States took a radical departure from the Commonwealth system at the Revolution. From the beginning, the courts-martial system was placed under the firm control of the legislative branch, which was given the enumerated power to make regulations to govern the military. The structural placement of courts-martial within our system determines the degree of judicial independence and due process rights they will receive; as legislative courts, they must offer fundamental due process and such other protections as Congress may statutorily provide. Legislative courts are not constitutionally required to provide all the protections of an Article III court, indeed, such protections would be inimical to their existence, for, as one scholar has observed, "Article III litigation is a rather grand and very expensive affair," cumbersome and inefficient.[468] The very nature of a legislative court involves a compromise between individual rights and Congress's ability to exercise its enumerated powers under the Constitution.

Thus, it is important to avoid the superficial appeal of changing our military justice system merely because our close allies have done so. Their governing charters require all criminal tribunals to use the same standards. In contrast, our Constitutional structure of

---

[468] Bator, *supra* note 241, at 262.

government places courts-martial on a different footing than civilian tribunals. So long as Congress continues to exercise its enumerated Constitutional power to provide for the government of the armed forces, the military justice system will necessarily be subject to a different standard than that employed in the Article III federal courts.

C. Changing the Rules Through Judicial Activism

1. The Strategy: Use the Implied Bias Doctrine to Change the Rules for Panel Member Selection

In recent months, an activist majority of the CAAF has opened a new front in the war against discretionary convening authority selection of panel members. *United States v. Wiesen*[469] demonstrates that the CAAF majority is willing to use the court's implied bias doctrine in a way that effectively rewrites UCMJ Article 25(d)(2), burdening convening authorities with a requirement to consider actual and potential command and supervisory relationships when appointing panel members.

The issue in *Wiesen* involved a defense challenge for cause on the court-martial president, Colonel (COL) Williams, who commanded the 2d Brigade of the 3d Infantry Division (Mechanized) at Fort Stewart, Georgia. Voir dire revealed that COL Williams had

---

[469] 56 M.J. 172 (2001), *pet. for recons. denied*, 57 M.J. 48 (2001). The accused in *Wiesen* was convicted by a general court-martial comprised of officer and enlisted members of two specifications of attempted forcible sodomy with a child, indecent acts with a child, and obstruction of justice. He was sentenced to a dishonorable discharge, twenty years' confinement, total forfeitures of pay and allowances, and reduction to the grade of E-1. *Wiesen*, 56 M.J. at 172.

either an actual or potential command relationship over six other members of the panel.[470]

All together, those members and COL Williams formed the two-thirds majority necessary to convict the accused.[471] The military judge thoroughly explored the issue of potential bias on the record. The court martial president and all other panel members stated on the record, under oath, that this senior/subordinate relationship would not affect their ability to deliberate and vote.[472] The defense counsel challenged COL Williams for cause on the grounds of implied bias. Based on the answers to voir dire questions, and, undoubtedly, his observation of the demeanor of the members, the military judge denied the challenge.[473] The defense counsel used a peremptory challenge on the panel president to preserve the issue for appeal.[474]

---

[470] COL Williams had direct authority over four members of the panel who were part of his brigade: two battalion commanders, a battalion executive officer, and a company first sergeant. Two other members of the panel--a forward support battalion commander and his command sergeant major--were from his brigade combat team (BCT). In an Army division, major subordinate commands include maneuver brigades (such as armor or mechanized infantry brigades), a divisional artillery brigade, a brigade-size division support command, and other units. A maneuver brigade typically consists of three battalions. When a maneuver brigade deploys, other divisional units are attached, or "sliced" to it to form a BCT. Those units, which include artillery and forward support battalions, may train with the maneuver brigade but are not part of its command structure in a garrison environment. Thus, in garrison, COL Williams would only directly command, supervise, and rate members of his maneuver brigade. The forward support battalion commander and sergeant major would be commanded and rated by the commander of the division support command. In its petition for reconsideration, the Government alleged that the CAAF had not paid sufficient attention to the actual command and supervisory arrangements at Fort Stewart. In denying the petition for reconsideration, the majority seemed to suggest that it didn't care: "Although our opinion did not comment on the specifics of each supervisory relationship or the operational status of each brigade at Fort Stewart, *those particular facts were not critical to our finding that the military judge abused his discretion in denying the challenge for cause*." *Wiesen II*, 57 M.J. at 49 (emphasis added).

[471] *Wiesen*, 56 M.J. at 175.

[472] *Id.* at 175.

[473] *Id.* at 174.

[474] *Id.* The R.C.M. requires that the challenging party preserve denied challenges for cause by using a peremptory challenge against the denied individual:

On appeal, the Army Court of Criminal Appeals (ACCA) affirmed.[475] Over vigorous dissents from Chief Judge Crawford and Senior Judge Sullivan,[476] Judge Baker, writing for a bare majority of the CAAF, reversed, holding that the military judge had abused his discretion in denying the challenge for cause.[477] The majority found that "where a panel member has a supervisory position over enough other members to make up the two-thirds majority necessary to convict, "we are placing an intolerable strain on public perception of the military justice system."[478] Because of the potential impact on the military justice system, the Government petitioned for reconsideration. In a per curiam opinion, the same majority denied the petition,[479] again over the separate dissents of Judges Crawford and Sullivan.

> [W]hen a challenge for cause is denied, a peremptory challenge by the challenging party against any member shall preserve the issues for later review, provided that when the member who was unsuccessfully challenged for cause is peremptorily challenged by the same party, that party must state that it would have exercised its peremptory challenge against another member if the challenge for cause had been granted.

MCM, *supra* note 5, R.C.M. 912(f)(4). The real irony of Wiesen is that the panel that eventually convicted and sentenced the accused to twenty years' confinement no longer included COL Williams.

[475] *Id.* at 177 (noting that the decision of the ACCA is reversed). There is no ACCA opinion available in *Wiesen*.

[476] Judge Crawford's dissent focused on two primary areas, the disconnect between the CAAF's implied bias doctrine and the fundamentally different implied bias doctrine in the federal courts, and the weaknesses of the majority's perception of the American public. *See id.* at 177-81 (Crawford, C.J., dissenting). Judge Sullivan's dissent criticized the majority for invading the province of Congress and the President by, in effect, engaging in judicial legislation or judicial rulemaking. *See id.* at 181-185 (Sullivan, J., dissenting).

[477] *Id.*

[478] *Id.*

[479] United States v. Wiesen, 57 M.J. 48, 50 (2002) [hereinafter *Wiesen II*].

The foundation for the majority's opinion was the CAAF's implied-bias doctrine, derived from R.C.M. 912(f)(1)(N), which provides that a member shall be excused for cause "whenever it appears that the member . . . . Should not sit as a member in the interest of having the court-martial free from substantial doubt as to legality, fairness, and impartiality."[480] As developed by the CAAF's case law over the years, the doctrine seeks to "view the situation [as to whether a member should sit] through the eyes of the public, focusing on the appearance of fairness."[481] This is a nebulous standard at best, and one that in the *Wiesen* majority's own words, the CAAF has "struggled to define . . . or just disagreed on what that scope should be."[482] *Wiesen* demonstrates that the struggle continues.

The *Wiesen* majority opinion fails to provide an objective, coherent analytical framework for analyzing implied bias. Without providing any standards for determining how to view the case "through the eyes of the public," the majority simply strung together a series of speculative statements on its perceptions of public opinion.[483] The majority believes that the public trusts the integrity of military officers to abide by their oaths, in and out of the deliberation room.[484] The problem is that the public, which understands that military

---

[480] MCM, *supra* note 5, R.C.M. 912(f)(1)(N).

[481] *See* United States v. Rome, 47 M.J. 467, 469 (1998).

[482] *See Wiesen*, 56 M.J. at 175.

[483] The majority's language richly illustrates this point. Speculative phrases such as "public perception . . . may nonetheless be affected," "[f]or lack of a more precise term," "simply too high a risk that the public will perceive," *see id.* at 176, are the order of the day. The majority also appears to be aware that its failure to use objective standards opens up the opinion for criticism, blustering, "This is not 'knowing it when you see it,' or appellate judges attempting to extrapolate 'public perceptions' from the bench." *Id.* Of course, that is precisely what the majority opinion does. A rose by any other name is still a rose.

[484] *Id.* at 176.

personnel lead, command, and follow each other, might wonder to what extent institutional military deference for senior officers would come into play in the deliberation room.[485] When a senior officer supervises a high enough percentage of the panel, it establishes "the wrong atmosphere,"[486] creating "simply too high a risk that the public will perceive that the accused received something less than a jury of ten equal members, although something more than a jury of one."[487] Nothing in the opinion assists military justice practitioners in determining how to measure public perception of the justice system; there is not, for example, a "reasonable person" test of the kind so familiar in American appellate jurisprudence.[488]

The majority further complicated matters for the practitioner by shifting the burden of proof for causal challenges of panel members based on implied bias from the accused to the Government. [489] The majority adopted a standard requiring the government to demonstrate

---

[485] *Id.*

[486] *Id.*

[487] *Id.*

[488] Indeed, Chief Judge Crawford made this point in her dissent in *Wiesen II*. She stated that implied-bias should be measured by the "long-standing legal standard of the 'reasonable person test.' A 'reasonable person' is a person 'knowing all the facts' and circumstances surrounding the issue in the case, including the rationales of the UCMJ and the Manual for Courts-Martial." *Wiesen II*, 57 M.J. at 54 (Crawford, C.J., dissenting). The public of the *Wiesen* majority's opinion is ignorant, uninformed, opinionated, and reactionary.

[489] The normal burden of proof for causal challenges is on the party making the challenge. *See* MCM, *supra* note 5, R.C.M. 912(f)(3).

the necessity for the challenged member to serve on the panel because of "operational deployments or needs."[490]

2. Response: The Theoretical Shortcomings and Practical Drawbacks of Wiesen

The *Wiesen* majority opinion reveals the limitations of an appellate court in determining public opinion. Without fact-finding ability, investigative resources, or a constituency to provide input,[491] an appellate court is left to its imagination in trying to determine how the public might view a particular practice in the military justice system. Most critically, an appellate court has no way to measure the impact of its decisions on the military; this is one of the primary reasons for the military deference doctrine in the Article III courts.[492] When an appellate court ventures into the domain of the legislature, the consequences to the military can be particularly serious:

---

[490] *Wiesen*, 56 M.J. at 176. The majority's language on the issue is quite clear: "Here, deployed units may have diminished the potential pool of members, but the Government failed to demonstrate that it was necessary for the Brigade Commander to serve on this panel." *Id.* In its denial of the Government's petition for reconsideration, the majority stated it had never shifted the burden, but had merely suggested that the Government could have used these factors in rebuttal to demonstrate the necessity of the Brigade Commander's service. *Wiesen II*, 57 M.J. at 49. However, the majority undercut this assertion in the next paragraph when it stated, "Notwithstanding the operational requirements at the time, there remained ample officers at Fort Stewart from which to select a member other than the Brigade Commander." *Id.* at 50. While this might, perhaps, have been true, UCMJ art. 25(d)(2) leaves that decision to the convening authority, not the CAAF

[491] *Cf.* ABNER J. MIKVA & ERIC LANE, AN INTRODUCTION TO STATUTORY INTERPRETATION AND THE LEGISLATIVE PROCESS 68-84 (1997). Mikva and Lane point out that three primary factors make the legislative process legitimate: deliberativeness, or the structures and steps of the process that slow legislative decision-making and remove it from the passions, immediacy, and prevailing desires of legislators or constituencies; representativeness, which requires legislators to stay in touch with the people they represent; and accessibility, which guarantees an open legislative process. *Id.* Through the use of committees and hearings, the legislature is able to investigate and gather information from a wide variety of sources regarding the impact and scope of proposed legislation. *See id.* at 90-94. In addition, legislators have significant staff resources available to assist them. *See id.* at 95.

[492] *See supra* note 288 and accompanying text.

A mistaken judicial conclusion that servicemen's individual rights can be protected without impairing military efficiency has the court do inadvertently what it has no standard for doing deliberately. *Because the uses to which the armed forces are put cannot be judged by the principles of the legal system, mistaken balancing that impairs those uses is not offset by vindication of the hierarchy of values within the system.*[493]

Issues of courts-martial panel composition fall squarely within the legislative purview of Congress and the rule-making authority of the President.[494] As Judge Crawford noted in her dissent to the CAAF's denial of reconsideration in *Wiesen*, Congress made all commissioned officers eligible to serve on courts-martial panels, making no exclusion for officers who were rated by another member of the panel.[495] In his dissent, Judge Sullivan was even more specific:

Congress *could have provided* that a member shall be disqualified if he or she is a military commander of a significant number of the members of the panel. Congress has been aware that, for years, commanders have sat on panels with their subordinates. *Congress could have prohibited this situation by law but failed to do so.* A court should not judicially legislate when Congress, in its wisdom, does not.[496]

What the CAAF majority accomplished in *Wiesen* was a judicial revision of UCMJ Article 25(d)(2). UCMJ Article 25(d)(2) requires a convening authority to select best-qualified members by criteria of age, experience, education, training, length of service and judicial temperament. In effect, *Wiesen* has rewritten Article 25(d)(2) to require convening

---

[493] Hirshhorn, *supra* note 284, at 238.

[494] *See* UCMJ art. 36 (2002) (establishing Presidential authority to make rules of procedure for courts-martial).

[495] *See Wiesen II*, 57 M.J. at 53 (Crawford, C.J., dissenting).

[496] *Id.* at 182 (Sullivan, J., dissenting) (citations omitted) (emphasis added).

authorities to consider, in addition to, or more likely in spite of, these requirements, "all the potential command and supervisory relationships of panel members in conjunction with final panel size and numbers needed for conviction." Furthermore, *Wiesen* has significantly changed the rules regarding challenges in implied bias cases, imposing new requirements on the Government to be prepared to justify panel selections in the light of operational needs.

Thus, *Wiesen* has a debilitating effect on the convening authority's discretion in panel selection. No longer may a convening authority select those whom he believes to be "best qualified" based on age, education, experience, training, length of service, and judicial temperament. Now he must consider who will sit on the panel with them, their relationships, and what potential command and supervisory arrangements will exist.[497] This potentially destroys a commander's authority to convene courts-martial in smaller commands, isolated installations, on ship, or in a deployed environment.[498]

---

[497] As of yet, there is no empirical evidence on the impact of *Wiesen* on the field. However, in an information paper, the Criminal Law Division of the Army Office of the Judge Advocate General noted that with the increased operational tempo of the Army and other services (at present, the Armed Services are engaged in combat in Iraq and Afghanistan), *Wiesen* is a "crippling precedent." Information Paper, Criminal Law Division, United States Army Office of the Judge Advocate General, subject: Rationale for Rule Changes in Light of *Armstrong* and *Wiesen* (6 December 2002) (on file with author). An alternative view is that *Wiesen* is merely a voir dire case that primarily places the burden on counsel and the bench to ensure that a panel never contains a majority sufficient to convict from the same chain of command. *See* Major Bradley J. Huestis, *New Developments in Pretrial Procedures: Evolution or Revolution*, 2002 ARMY. LAW. 20, 37 (Apr. 2002).

[498] Judge Crawford pointed to the potential impact of *Wiesen* on operations:

> The logical extension of the majority's view will make it very difficult for a deployed convening authority of a detached brigade, separate battalion, or units of similar size to convene a court-martial. This not only defeats the flexibility for which the UCMJ has provided since its inception, but also undermines good order and discipline in the armed services. If the commander of a brigade, separate battalion, or units of similar size of soldiers currently deployed in Asia wanted to convene a court-martial, he or she may practically be precluded from doing so without going outside the unit or changing venue. Either may impact on the mission.

There should be no doubt that the *Wiesen* majority intended to strike a blow at the convening authority's discretionary ability to appoint court-martial panel members. In the penultimate sentence of its per curiam denial of the Government's petition for reconsideration, the majority wrote, "The issue is appropriately viewed in the context of public perceptions of a system in which the commander who exercises prosecutorial discretion is the official who selects and structures the panel that will hear the case."[499] The *Wiesen* majority's true policy concern, then, hearkens back to the objections that Congress heard and considered when enacting the UCMJ over fifty years ago. Viewed in that context, *Wiesen* is a prime example of an activist appellate court arrogating to itself the power to change Constitutionally sound legislation with which it does not agree.[500]

Wiesen II, 57 M.J. at 55 (Crawford, C.J., dissenting).

[499] *Id.* at 50.

[500] Indeed, the majority's language also damns them in this matter. In an acid footnote responding to Judge Sullivan's dissent in the original opinion, the majority dismissed his concerns, cited *Marbury v. Madison*, and tartly observed, "The duty of judges is to say what the law is." In fact, *Marbury* says, "It is, emphatically, the province and duty of the judicial department, to say what the law is." Marbury v. Madison, 5 U.S. (1 Cranch) 137, 177-78 (1803). *Marbury* has never been a blank check to authorize appellate courts to rewrite statutes at their whim. In fact, it is doubtful *Marbury* has much application at all to the CAAF; as an Article I appellate court organized under the Department of Defense, the CAAF does not partake of the judicial power within the meaning of Article III. Moreover, to quote Lawrence Tribe, *Marbury* generally stands for the proposition that a federal court has power to refuse to give effect to congressional legislation if it is inconsistent with the Court's interpretation of the Constitution. *See* TRIBE, *supra* note 237, § 3-2, at 23. It is highly unlikely that *Marbury* means an Article I court can "say what the law is" by adding new requirements to congressional legislation when no constitutional issues have been raised.

IV. Counterattack: A Proposal to Solve the Problems of *Wiesen* and Shape the Future Debate on Convening Authority Panel Selection

This section proposes a two-phase strategy to aggressively counter efforts to remove the convening authority from panel member selection. The first phase, the "close fight,"[501] involves taking steps to solve the problems created by the CAAF in *United States v. Wiesen*. This can most effectively be done using the rule-making authority Congress granted the President in Article 36 of the UCMJ. The second phase, "the deep fight,"[502] recognizes that defenders of the current system cannot hope to prevail in a public debate in which the military justice system is subjected to misleading and incomplete comparisons with the civilian criminal justice system. The solution is to change the terms of the debate, pointing out the purposes of military justice, its historical and constitutional validity, and most important, the benefits to the military and the accused of a system in which the convening authority uses his discretion to select a panel of the most highly qualified members of his command.

---

[501] According to U.S. Army doctrine, close operations, or the "close fight," are those in which forces are "in immediate contact with the enemy and the fighting between the committed forces and the readily available tactical reserves of both combatants." *See* U.S. DEP'T OF ARMY, FIELD MANUAL 101-5-1, OPERATIONAL TERMS AND GRAPHICS 1-28 (30 Sep. 1997) [hereinafter FM 101-5-1].

[502] Deep operations, or "the deep fight," "employ long-range fires, air and ground maneuver, and command and control warfare to defeat the enemy by denying him freedom of action; disrupting his preparation for battle and his support structure; and disrupting or destroying the coherence and tempo of his operations." *See id.* at 1-47. The purpose of deep operations is to shape the battlefield for future operations.

A. The Close Fight: Wrestling With *Wiesen*

As previously mentioned, the CAAF's decision in *Wiesen* has been, thus far, the most effective of contemporary attacks against the convening authority's role. This is because the CAAF exercises an important supervisory role over the military justice system. Its opinions are entitled to great deference, and history has demonstrated that commanders and staff judge advocates will change their military justice practices in order to satisfy the standards handed down by the CAAF. But the CAAF exceeds its jurisdictional mandate when its decisions usurp functions that belong to other branches of government.[503] In this case, the effect of CAAF's decision is to impose a new statutory element on UCMJ Article 25(d)(2), a function that belongs not to an appellate court but to Congress.

There are several potential responses to *Wiesen*. The first is simply to accept it, making appropriate modifications to panel selection procedures or placing the burden on trial counsel to avoid *Wiesen* problems during the voir dire and challenges phase of trial. The second is for the Government to seek certiorari from the United States Supreme Court. A third option is for the President to use his rule-making authority under UCMJ Article 36 to amend R.C.M. 503(a) and R.C.M. 912(f)(1)(N), making clear his intent that command and supervisory

---

[503] The CAAF has overreached before. A few years ago, the CAAF attempted to use the All Writs Act to enjoin the Secretary of the Air Force from dropping an Air Force officer from the rolls. The Supreme Court ruled that the CAAF did not have the authority under the All Writs Act to enjoin the Secretary of the Air Force from taking an administrative personnel action against an Air Force officer. The All Writs Act could not give the CAAF jurisdiction it did not have. *See* Clinton v. Goldsmith, 526 U.S. 529 (1999). Writing for the majority, Justice Souter noted that Congress had limited the CAAF's jurisdiction to act only with respect to review of sentences imposed by courts-martial. *Id.* at 534.

relationships are no impediment to a convening authority's discretion in appointing panel members. Each of these options will be discussed in turn.

1. Option One: Accept Wiesen and Its Effects on Military Justice System

Under this option, the military would accept the results of *Wiesen* and modify its practices accordingly. Some jurisdictions would read the case as limiting the convening authority's discretion in appointing panel members and create mechanisms to ensure no panels would suffer from a potential *Wiesen* problem. Other jurisdictions would make no changes to panel selection procedures, instead viewing *Wiesen* simply as a voir-dire-and-challenges case[504] and placing the burden on trial counsel to be especially vigilant during the voir dire phase of a court-martial, joining in defense challenges for cause to ensure that the final composition of any panel would not violate the *Wiesen* rule that the two-thirds majority of the panel necessary to convict could not fall under the potential command or supervision of the panel president.

The fallacy of simply accepting *Wiesen* is that either of the above approaches will damage the military justice system. In jurisdictions that view *Wiesen* as applying to the selection and appointment of court-martial panels, similar issues may never arise at trial because the panels will already have been screened, shuffled, and sifted to comply with *Wiesen*. However, the paucity of such issues will stem not from the inherent virtues of

---

[504] Indeed, there is by no means universal agreement that *Wiesen* sounds the death knell for the commander's role in the military justice system. Some, in fact, view *Wiesen* primarily as a voir dire case. *See* Huestis, *supra* note 497, at 37.

117

Wiesen, but because of the limiting effect the case has on a convening authority's discretion. The price to be paid is judicial evisceration of the UCMJ Article 25(d)(2) subjective selection criteria.

Jurisdictions that do not change panel selection procedures to comply with *Wiesen* will be vulnerable to creative defense strategies during voir dire and challenges. For example, taking advantage of the CAAF's mandate that trial judges should liberally grant challenges for cause,[505] a defense counsel could selectively challenge panel members, shaping the panel so it violates *Wiesen* even as it approaches minimum quorum requirements.[506] At that point, the defense would be able to make an additional challenge for cause because of the *Wiesen*

---

[505] *See* United States v. White, 36 M.J. 284, 287 (C.M.A. 1993) (instructing military judges liberally to grant defense challenges for cause).

[506] This would not be especially difficult to do. The following hypothetical presents just one of many possible panel arrangements that would be potentially vulnerable to manipulation by defense counsel. Assume that Fort Hypothetical has two major subordinate commands, A Brigade and B Brigade, each commanded by an O-6. Suppose that the commanding general of Fort Hypothetical appoints a ten-member officer-and-enlisted general court-martial panel. For each rank represented on the panel, there is one member from A Brigade and one member from B Brigade. No members of the court-martial panel are from the same battalion. The panel consists of two O-6 brigade commanders, two O-5 battalion commanders, two O-4 battalion staff officers, two E-9 battalion command sergeants major, and two E-8 company first sergeants. At PFC Snuffy's general court-martial for several counts of barracks larceny, the defense counsel is aware of *Wiesen* and plans her strategy accordingly. She challenges the commander of A Brigade for cause because PFC Snuffy is a member of A Brigade and the commander had read the blotter report, appointed an Article 32 investigation, and forwarded the charges with a recommendation for disposition. She challenges the battalion commander from A Brigade because in past dealings with her, the commander had formed a negative opinion of her advocacy and had complained about her to the installation chief of justice. She challenges a sergeant major from A Brigade because he knew about the offense, had formed an opinion concerning the accused's guilt, and had sent an e-mail to the other sergeants major in the brigade warning them to watch out for barracks thieves. She challenges a first sergeant from B Brigade because of what she perceives as his inflexible attitude towards the offense of barracks larceny. Using the liberal grant mandate, the judge grants the four challenges, leaving a six-member panel. The panel president is the O-6 B Brigade commander. Also from B Brigade are an O-5 battalion commander, an O-4 battalion staff officer, and an E-9 battalion command sergeant major. The remaining members are an O-4 staff officer and an E-8 first sergeant from A Brigade. The B Brigade commander is in the rating chain for each of the B Brigade members (rater for the battalion commander, senior rater for the battalion staff officer and the command sergeant major). The panel now violates *Wiesen* because four of its six members (the two-thirds majority necessary to convict) are part of the panel president's rating chain.

problem its earlier challenges created.[507] If the granted challenge reduces the panel to its

minimum for a quorum, the defense could potentially "bust" the panel by exercising a

peremptory challenge on one of the remaining members. If the challenge is denied, defense

could preserve the issue for appellate review by exercising a peremptory challenge against

the senior member of the panel.[508] Either way, the Government loses. Jurisdictions that

ignore *Wiesen* when selecting and appointing panel members may well see it come back to

haunt them later in the form of "busted" panels or, possibly, reversals and re-hearings. The

cost to the system in terms of efficiency and utility to the command could prove onerous. At

smaller installations or aboard ship, the system could grind to a halt.

In time, the CAAF itself could limit *Wiesen* to its facts or otherwise distance itself from

the opinion. However, as the development of the CAAF's implied bias doctrine

demonstrates,[509] the likelihood is that *Wiesen* will become the basis for further

---

[507] The R.C.M. specifically permits challenges for cause even after initial examination and challenges of the members, providing that "A challenge for cause may be made at any other time during trial when it becomes apparent that a ground for challenge may exist. Such examination of the member and presentation of evidence as may be necessary may be made in order to resolve the matter." MCM, *supra* note 5, R.C.M. 912(f)(2)(B). Thus, if a *Wiesen* problem arises only after the exercise of challenges for cause pursuant to R.C.M. 912(f)(2)(A), counsel would be able to raise the issue at that point.

Returning to the Fort Hypothetical case, the Government's problem becomes apparent. The defense counsel could now challenge the panel president for cause. The Government, in fact, could join in the challenge for cause so as to avoid the *Wiesen* issue. If the challenge is successful, the panel now contains five members and the defense counsel, with her peremptory challenge intact, can "bust" the panel and force the convening authority to detail new members. *Id.* R.C.M. 505(c)(2)(B). If she loses, the defense counsel can preserve the issue for appeal by using her peremptory on the brigade commander

[508] *See id.* R.C.M. 912(f)(4) (stating that in order to preserve a challenge for review, the accused must exercise a peremptory against the member and then announce that he would have used the peremptory against someone else but for the denied challenge).

[509] Over the course of five years, the CAAF went from questioning whether its version of the implied bias doctrine even existed, *see* United States v. Dinatale, 44 M.J. 325, 329 (1996) ("I write only to question if there is such a thing as 'implied bias.'") (Cox, C.J., concurring), to enshrining it as a well-established principle of

encroachments on a convening authority's discretion. Implied bias based on potential rating schemes could morph into implied bias based on the position or seniority of panel members. For example, if a convening authority seeks to avoid *Wiesen* problems by appointing his chief of staff to panels in lieu of senior O-6 commanders,[510] one can easily imagine the court expanding the implied bias doctrine to include individuals who serve as the "alter ego" or right-hand-man to the commander. The court could also invalidate a panel that included too many O-6 commanders because of their tendency to outrank, take charge of, lead, and be granted deference to by lower-ranking members of the panel.[511] Because *Wiesen* lacks a coherent analytical framework, its potential scope is limited only by the unique fact patterns arising in various jurisdictions and the creativity of defense counsel in raising novel challenges.

2. Option Two: Seek Certiorari from the United States Supreme Court

Article 67a of the UCMJ permits either the Government or the accused to seek review of CAAF decisions by writ of certiorari.[512] The Government could apply for a writ of certiorari,

---

military jurisprudence, *see* United States v. Rome, 47 M.J. 467, 469 (1998) (stating that R.C.M. 912 includes both actual and implied bias), to using the doctrine to create the result in *Wiesen*.

[510] Typically, an installation or division chief of staff would not be in the rating chain for officers and enlisted from the major subordinate commands.

[511] This result would be not at all inconsistent with the *Wiesen* majority, which seemed concerned that an objective public might ask to what extent deference for senior leaders comes into play in the deliberation room. "The public perceives accurately that military commissioned and noncommissioned officers are expected to lead, not just manage; to command, not just direct; and to follow, not just get out of the way." *Wiesen*, 56 M.J. at 176.

[512] UCMJ art. 67a states:

> (a) Decisions of the United States Court of Appeals for the Armed Forces are subject to review by the Supreme Court by writ of certiorari as provided in section 1259 of Title 28.

seeking to invalidate the CAAF's implied bias doctrine as applied in *Wiesen*. If the Government were successful both in obtaining the writ and on appeal, the authority and finality of a Supreme Court ruling invalidating the CAAF's implied bias doctrine would go a long way toward preserving the practice of discretionary convening authority appointment of court-martial panel members.

There are two potential drawbacks associated with this course of action. The first is that the Court could refuse, without explanation, to grant certiorari. Although this would not have the legal effect of blessing the CAAF's decision in *Wiesen*,[513] as a practical matter, a denial of certiorari would help buttress the opinion. The Government, having expended the energy and political capital to petition for certiorari,[514] would not likely try again on a similar issue unless there is an especially compelling set of facts. On the other hand, a denial of certiorari could serve to embolden the CAAF, ultimately leading to further expansion of the implied bias doctrine and additional judicially created limitations on the subjective selection criteria of UCMJ Article 25(d)(2).

The Supreme Court may not review by a writ of certiorari under this section any action by the Court of Appeals for the Armed Forces in refusing to grant a petition for review.

UCMJ Art. 67a (2002).

[513] Because a writ of certiorari is discretionary, a denial of certiorari generally carries no implication whatever regarding the Court's view of the merits of the case on which it has denied review. Tribe, *supra* note 237, at 44 n.9 (quoting Maryland v. Baltimore Radio Show, Inc., 333 U.S. 912, 917-19 (1950)).

[514] The services do not have direct access to the Supreme Court but must first persuade the Solicitor General, by way of the Department of Defense General Counsel, to take the case. *See* Rotunda and Nowak, *supra* note 267, at § 2.2, for a discussion of the role of the Solicitor General. By law, only the Solicitor General or his designee can conduct and argue cases in which the United States has an interest before the Supreme Court. *Id.* (citing 28 U.S.C.A. § 518(a)). Consequently, the military does not lightly seek certiorari from the Court. *Cf.* E-mail from Major Bradley Huestis, Professor, The Judge Advocate General's School, U.S. Army, to CPT Chris Behan, Student, 51st Graduate Course, The Judge Advocate General's School, U.S. Army (25 Nov. 2002) (containing a string of e-mail traffic in which the various participants in the process of trying to obtain certiorari discuss the *Wiesen* case) (on file with author).

The second problem is potentially the most dangerous: The Court could grant certiorari and affirm *Wiesen*. This could occur because of the Court's long-standing practice of settling issues on the narrowest grounds possible.[515] Although *Wiesen* has a potentially deleterious effect on the commander's role in the military justice system, there is no developed record or empirical evidence to demonstrate that effect, and one could not be created merely for the sake of a Supreme Court appeal. All issues related to impact on the system or *Wiesen's* practical effect of rewriting UCMJ Article 25(d)(2) would have to be presented as hypothetical problems and could run afoul of the Court's practice of avoiding advisory opinions.[516]

Furthermore, the CAAF has framed its implied bias doctrine not as an issue of statutory interpretation but rather as a natural outgrowth of the Rules for Courts-Martial, which permit challenges if a member "should not sit as a member in the interest of having the court-martial free from substantial doubt as to legality, fairness, and impartiality."[517] On the narrow issue of whether the CAAF's implied bias doctrine effectuates the President's intent to hold fair and impartial courts-martial, it is quite possible that the Court could defer to the CAAF's judgment on the matter and affirm. Such an opinion would substantially limit the military's options for overcoming *Wiesen*.

---

[515] *See* Rotunda and Nowak, *supra* note 267, at § 2.13 (discussing the Court's desire to settle issues on the narrowest possible grounds so as to avoid having to decide Constitutional issues).

[516] According to Rotunda and Nowak, there are four primary reasons the Court declines to give advisory opinions. First, they may not be binding on the parties. Second, advisory opinions undermine the basic theory behind the adversary system. Third, advisory opinions unnecessarily force the Court to reach and decide complex constitutional issues. Fourth, the power to render advisory opinions is thought to be beyond the scope of what the Framers intended. *See id.*

[517] MCM, *supra* note 5, R.C.M. 912(f)(1)(N).

Of the three possible outcomes of a petition for certiorari, the two most likely to occur are the least desirable from the Government's point of view. The third--a grant of certiorari followed by a favorable ruling--is not worth risking the other two possibilities.

3. Option Three: Change the Manual for Courts-Martial

Because the CAAF has based its implied bias doctrine on the Rules for Courts-Martial rather than employing a statutory or Constitutional analysis, the best option for overruling *Wiesen* is to change the Rules. If the President clearly expresses a policy that command and supervisory relationships neither disqualify members from sitting nor form the basis for a viable challenge for cause, the CAAF will be forced either to retreat from its implied bias doctrine or to shift the basis of its analysis to a Constitutional or statutory interpretation. Should that occur in a future case, the Government would be in a better position to seek certiorari and prevail at the Supreme Court.

Congress has specifically granted the President the authority to promulgate procedural and evidentiary rules for courts-martial in Article 36 of the UCMJ.[518] There is, furthermore, a strong argument that the President has inherent power to promulgate such rules stemming

---

[518] UCMJ Article 36(a) provides:

> Pretrial, trial, and post-trial procedures, including modes of proof, for cases arising under this chapter triable in courts-martial, military commissions and other military tribunals, and procedures for courts of inquiry, may be prescribed by the President by regulations which shall, so far as he considers practicable, apply the principles of law and the rules of evidence generally recognized in the trial of criminal cases in the United States district courts, but which may not be contrary to or inconsistent with this chapter.

UCMJ Art. 36(a) (2002).

from his Constitutional authority as Commander-in-Chief of the armed forces.[519] In Articles 18 and 56 of the UCMJ, Congress has also authorized the President to set maximum punishment limits for violations of the punitive articles of the UCMJ.[520] The rules and punishment limitations prescribed by the President are contained in the Manual for Courts-Martial (Manual).

The Manual consists of five parts--a Preamble, the Rules for Courts-Martial, the Military Rules of Evidence, and the Punitive Articles of the UCMJ--that have been created through executive orders in accordance with the President's Article 36 authority.[521] Those provisions of the manual are binding on courts-martial practice. In addition, the Manual contains a number of supplementary materials, including discussion paragraphs and sections analyzing the Rules for Courts-Martial and the Military Rules of Evidence, which have been prepared by the Departments of Defense and Transportation.[522] The supplementary materials create

---

[519] U.S. CONST. ART. II, § 2. *See also* Captain Gregory E. Maggs, *Judicial Review of the* Manual for Courts-Martial, 160 MIL. L. REV. 96, 100-101 (1999) (discussing the statutory and constitutional basis for Presidential rule-making authority and observing that the President directed the conduct of courts-martial in the 19th century without specific statutory authority to do so).

[520] UCMJ art. 18 states, "[G]eneral courts-martial have jurisdiction to try persons subject to this chapter for any offense made punishable by this chapter and may, under such limitations as the President may prescribe, adjudge any punishment not forbidden by this chapter, including the penalty of death when specifically authorized by this chapter." UCMJ art. 18 (2002). UCMJ art. 56 states that "[t]he punishment which a court-martial may direct for an offense may not exceed such limits as the President may prescribe for that offense." UCMJ art. 56 (2002).

[521] *See* MCM, *supra* note 5, pt. I, ¶ 4 ("The Manual for Courts-Martial shall consist of this Preamble, the Rules for Courts-Martial, the Military rules of Evidence, the Punitive Articles, and Nonjudicial Punishment Procedures (Part I-V).").

[522] *See id.* Discussion.

no binding rights or responsibilities, but are a useful reference tool for practitioners and are

helpful in determining the intended meaning or effect of a Manual provision.[523]

The process of amending the Manual is relatively simple. If the President desires to

change or clarify the Manual for Courts-Martial, he does so by executive order.[524] The

President has, in fact, frequently amended the Manual over the years.[525] There is nothing in

---

[523] *See* Maggs, *supra* note 519, at 116-17. Maggs identifies three reasons that courts should not dismiss the supplementary materials in the Manual as irrelevant. First, the staff that prepared the materials has significant expertise in military law and actually drafted many of the rules in the Manual. Second, because of the sometimes limited access to research materials in the field, judge advocates often must rely on the supplementary materials in order to give advice to clients and commanders. Third, there is a long-standing judicial practice of deferring to an agency's own interpretation of the statutes it enforces. *See id.*

[524] In practice, of course, there is a deliberate process of amendment that ensures consensus among the services and other interested governmental agencies. In a treatise on court-martial procedure, Frances Gilligan and Fredric Lederer succinctly explain the process of *Manual* amendment:

> The Manual is kept current by the Joint Service Committee on Military Justice. This is a committee consisting of the officers responsible for criminal law in the armed forces (including the Coast Guard), augmented by representatives from the Department of Defense General Counsel's Office and the Court of Military Appeals. This body serves primarily as a policy-making one. The actual drafting work is customarily done by the Joint Service Committee on Military Justice Working Group, consisting of subordinates of the Committee's members. Changes may be initiated by the Working Group or drafted in response to the Committee's direction. No amendment is usually possible, however, without Committee endorsement. Proposed Manual changes must be coordinated with the Department of Transportation (because of the Coast Guard), the Attorney General and OMB. The President of course has the final decision. Changes in the Manual are inherently political, and absent unusual political machination, no change is likely to be made that does not have substantial backing, if not full consensus.

FRANCES A. GILLIGAN & FREDRIC I. LEDERER, 1 COURT-MARTIAL PROCEDURE § 1-54.00 n.137 (1991).

[525] *See generally,* MCM, *supra* note 5, at Appendix 25 (containing executive orders dating from 1984 that modified various provisions of the Manual). Of course, as with other areas of military justice, some reformers object to the current process of amending the Manual. In recent years, the Military Law Review has published an interesting debate on the issue. *Compare* Kevin J. Barry, *Modernizing the Manual for Courts-Martial Rule-Making Process: A Work in Progress,* 166 MIL. L. REV. 237 (2000) (suggesting that the Manual amendment process is flawed because it does not include input from a broad enough base of participants and suggesting adoption of a military judicial conference rule-making process) *with* Captain Gregory E. Maggs, *Cautious Skepticism About the Benefit of Adding More Formalities to the Manual for Courts-Martial Rule-Making Process: A Response to Captain Kevin J. Barry,* 166 MIL. L. REV. 1 (2000) (opining that Barry's suggested changes would yield little actual benefit to the rule-making process while imposing additional administrative burdens on the system) *and* Barry, *A Reply to Captain Gregory E. Maggs's "Cautious Skepticism Regarding*

the UCMJ or in the Manual itself that prevents the President from amending the Manual in order to clarify his policy in a manner that also happens to overrule a decision of the CAAF. Indeed, the power to amend the Manual provides the President with the ability to reign in the CAAF should its opinions hinder the efforts of the armed forces to make the military justice system work under actual conditions in the field. As one commentator has observed:

> The President, as Commander-in-Chief, is primarily responsible for the maintenance of order, morale, and discipline in the armed forces and the system of military justice is one of the principle means of maintaining them. It is essential to national safety that the President have sufficient power to make the system of military justice work effectively under the conditions which actually exist in the forces . . . .[526]

The simplest way to clarify the President's policy, uphold the statutory panel-selection provisions of the UCMJ, and overrule *Wiesen* is to amend Rules 503(a) and 912(f)(1)(N) of the Rules for Courts-Martial.[527] Amending the Manual permits the President to ensure that

---

Recommendations to Modernize the Manual for Courts-Martial Rule-Making Process, 166 MIL. L. REV. 37 (2000) (questioning the basis for Maggs's assertion and reiterating Barry's belief that the process must change).

[526] William R. Fratcher, *Presidential Power to Regulate Military Justice: A Critical Study of Decisions of the Court of Military Appeals*, 34 N.Y.U. L. REV. 861, 868 (1959), *quoted in* Maggs, *supra* note 519, at 110.

[527] The full text of the proposed rule changes, along with suggested discussion and analysis language, is at Appendix A. The proposals at Appendix A are adapted from two different proposals that have been considered by the Joint Services Committee for dealing with the problems created by *Wiesen*. The first proposal, from the DoD Office of the General Counsel, would have amended R.C.M. 912(f)(1)(N) and its discussion to clarify that the existence of a command or supervisory relationship between two or more members of a court-martial panel, even where such members constitute a majority sufficient to reach a finding of guilty, would not constitute grounds for a challenge for cause. E-mail from Major Bradley Huestis, Professor, The Judge Advocate General's School, U.S. Army, to CPT Chris Behan, Student, 51st Graduate Course, The Judge Advocate General's School, U.S. Army (25 Nov. 2002) (on file with author).

The second proposal, from the Criminal Law Department of the Office of the Judge Advocate General of the Army, was more sweeping and would have amended R.C.M. 503(a) to clarify that supervisory and command relationships do not disqualify members detailed to a court-martial; modified R.C.M. 912(f)(1) to make "actual bias" the standard for granting challenges for cause, as well as removing the discretionary language of R.C.M. 912(f)(1)(N) and replacing it with a list of non-discretionary criteria; and changed R.C.M. 912(f)(4) to conform military practice to the federal rules of procedure by eliminating the waiver rule that permits an accused to

the military justice system continues to operate efficiently in the field, while at the same time avoiding the potential drawbacks of seeking to overturn *Wiesen* in the Supreme Court or forcing the military justice system to modify its practices in accordance with *Wiesen*.

Rule 503(a) provides the procedures for detailing members. A new paragraph, R.C.M. 503(a)(4), would make clear that command or supervisory relationships are not disqualifying: "(4) *Members with a Command or Supervisory Relationship.* The Convening Authority may detail members with a command or supervisory relationship with other members and such relationships shall not disqualify any member from service on a court-martial panel." This rule would reflect pre-*Wiesen* practice and long-standing jurisprudence of both the COMA and the CAAF that senior-subordinate relationships, in and of themselves, do not automatically disqualify members from sitting on a panel.[528]

In order to further tighten up the provisions for challenging members, R.C.M. 912(f)(1)(N) should be amended by adding a second sentence: "The existence of a command or supervisory relationship between two or more members of a court-martial panel (even where such members constitute a majority sufficient to reach a finding of guilty) shall not constitute grounds for removal for cause." This sentence would specifically overrule *Wiesen*, support the subjective selection criteria of UCMJ Article 25(d)(2), and make clear a

---

preserve a challenge issue for appeal by using a peremptory challenge against a member who was unsuccessfully challenged for cause and stating that the peremptory would have been used against another member. Information Paper, Criminal Law Division, OTJAG, U.S. Army, subject: Rationale for Rule Changes in Light of *Armstrong* and *Wiesen* (6 Dec. 2002) (on file with author).

[528] *See, e.g.*, United States v. Bannworth, 36 M.J. 265, 268 (C.M.A. 1994) (holding that a senior-subordinate relationship between court members did not automatically disqualify the senior member from sitting on the panel).

Presidential policy that such relationships between panel members are an expected aspect of the military justice system. It would, moreover, support past rulings of the military appellate courts that senior-subordinate relationships, standing alone, are not a valid basis for a challenge for cause.[529] It would also preserve for trial and appellate courts the ability to exercise discretion and ensure that, within the policy constraints set by Congress and the President, the court-martial is "free from substantial doubt as to legality, fairness, and impartiality."[530]

If the President amends the Manual to overrule *Wiesen*, sound policy and principles would constrain the CAAF from holding the new Manual provision invalid. When a Manual provision does not conflict with the Constitution or the statutory provisions of the UCMJ, the appellate courts have generally shown great deference to the President.[531] Moreover, a court creates separation-of-powers issues when it purports to invalidate a policy choice that the President personally has made or approved.[532] The President not only has statutory authority to create rules to govern courts-martial, but he also has his inherent Constitutional powers as

---

[529] *See, e.g.*, United States v. Blocker, 32 M.J. 281, 286-87 (C.M.A. 1991) ("The mere fact of a rating relationship between members, like a senior-subordinate relationship, does not generally give rise to a challenge for cause.").

[530] MCM, *supra* note 5, R.C.M. 912(f)(1)(N). A rule change that requires actual bias and establishes a set list of mandatory criteria goes too far and could create potential Constitutional issues. Trial and appellate courts must retain a credible ability to watch over the military justice system and exercise discretion to ensure that the system meets contemporary standards of fairness and due process.

[531] *See* Maggs, *supra* note 519, at 105 n.48 (citing several cases in which the military appellate courts have expressed the principle that they should attempt to follow the President's intent in promulgating the Manual).

[532] *See id.* at 108-110. According to Maggs, there are three primary reasons that separation of powers principles apply when the appellate courts invalidate provisions of the Manual. First, executive orders necessarily embody policy choices because the President has complete control over their contents. Second, Congress has assigned to the President the task of creating rules and has invested some discretion in him. Third, the President and his advisers have special knowledge about the needs and concerns of the military that is not available to appellate courts. *See id.*

Commander-in-Chief. Thus, appellate courts should not lightly disturb clear expressions of Presidential policy in the Manual.

In summary, amending the Manual for Courts-Martial presents the simplest and most effective method of solving the problems *Wiesen* has created for the military justice system.[533] The proposed rules are consistent with the UCMJ, past practice in the military, and the needs of a system that must be effective under a wide variety of conditions worldwide. Furthermore, they clearly articulate a Presidential policy that appellate courts will find difficult to tamper with in future cases.

B. The Deep Fight: Changing the Terms of the Debate

The current debate on the role of the convening authority in the military justice system is cast in terms that place military justice in an unflattering light. The American military justice system has been depicted as the dinosaur of all modern civilian and military justice systems, an anachronism that stubbornly clings to the outmoded idea of personal command involvement in critical matters of justice at the expense of the individual.[534] Ironically, proponents of change have not been able to mount successful attacks on the actual fairness of

---

[533] Reformers have also recognized the utility of amending the Manual in order to affect the panel selection system. Kevin Barry, for instance, has suggested that the Manual might be amended to require random selection of courts-martial panel members. *See* Barry, *A Reply to Captain Maggs's "Cautious Skepticism"*, *supra* note 525, at 48-49 ("To suggest that improvements in the system of selection of court-members could not, or should not, or would not be expected to come by regulation, is to ignore what has seemed not only possible and plausible, but also necessary, to numerous commentators."). There is certainly no harm in beating the reformers at their own game and amending the Manual to counteract the CAAF's erosion of the Constitutionally sound and eminently useful practice of discretionary convening authority panel selection.

[534] *See generally* Barry, *supra* note 22 (claiming that the U.S. military justice system once led the world but now has fallen sadly behind).

the system; indeed, the statutory protections of the UCMJ doom such attacks to failure. It is the perception of bias or unfairness they attack. By framing the debate in terms of perception rather than reality, reformers are able to avoid the inconvenience of empirical or factual support for their premise that the system "looks bad" and must change. Defenders of the system are therefore placed at a profound disadvantage, forced to fight on terms of the opposition's choosing.

It is time to change the terms of the debate to include a discussion of how reforms match up with the constitutional framework and operational mission of the military justice system. Congress created the American military justice system as a legislative court system in furtherance of its enumerated Constitutional power to make rules for the government of the military.[535] The modern UCMJ was designed as a legislative compromise to provide individual rights while still retaining the paramount role of the commander in administering military justice.[536] In the Preamble to the Manual for Courts-Martial, the President has declared, "The purpose of military law is to promote justice, to assist in maintaining good order and discipline in the armed forces, to promote efficiency and effectiveness in the military establishment, and thereby to strengthen the national security of the United States."[537]

---

[535] *See supra* Part II.D.

[536] *See supra* Part II.C.3.

[537] MCM, *supra* note 5, part I, ¶ 3.

Instead of asking how the military justice system stacks up in comparison to the military justice systems from other political traditions or even the American civilian criminal jury system, the debate should be framed in terms of how proposed changes match the Congressional values embodied in the UCMJ and the President's declaration of the purposes for military justice. If a proposed change reduces efficiency, adds complexity, and degrades the ability of American commanders to promote good order and discipline in the armed forces, it matters little that the change brings the military justice system closer to an idealized concept of justice. Congress long ago rejected the idea that the "justice" element outweighs the "military" element of military justice.[538]

In furtherance of that end, this section will address the theoretical and practical reasons that command involvement in the appointment of court members is critical to our military justice system. First, the section will discuss the legal responsibilities shouldered by the commander and the effect that removing his authority over the military justice system would have. Closely related to this is the role of the military justice system in wartime and the necessity of retaining command involvement under conditions of combat or similar exigencies. Second, the section will examine the benefits that service members enjoy as a result of command appointment of court members. When the debate on the practice of

---

[538] In its report on the UCMJ, the House Committee on Armed Services specifically addressed the balance between an idealistic concept of justice and operational reality:

> We cannot escape the fact that the law which we are now writing will be as applicable and must be as workable in time of war as in time of peace, and regardless of any desires which may stem from an idealistic conception of justice, we must avoid the enactment of provisions which will unduly restrict those who are responsible for the conduct of our military operations.

House Report, *supra* note 210, at 8.

convening authority selection of panel members is framed in terms of its benefits to the military hierarchy and the individual service-member, it becomes apparent that command involvement is critical in maintaining the distinctive military character of the military justice system and that current practices are superior to proposals for reform.

1. How Discretionary Selection of Panel Members Benefits the Command

As a threshold matter, it is important to recognize one of the hard truths about the military justice system that is often left unsaid: there is no point in its existence if it cannot meet the needs of military commanders. General of the Army Dwight D. Eisenhower testified to this effect before a meeting of the New York Lawyers' Club in 1948, in the midst of the debates on the Uniform Code of Military Justice:

> I know that groups of lawyers in examining the legal procedures in the Army have believed that it would be very wise to observe, in the Army and in the Armed Services in general, that great distinction that is made in our Government organization, of a division of power. . . . But I should like to call your attention to one fact about the Army, about the Armed Services. *It was never set up to insure justice.* It is set up as a servant, a servant, of the civilian population of this country to do a job, to perform a particular function; and that function, in its successful performance, demands within the Army somewhat, almost of a violation of the very concepts upon which our government is established. . . . *So this division of command responsibility and the responsibility for the adjudication of offenses and of accused offenders cannot be as separate as it is in our own democratic government.*[539]

---

[539] Sherman, *supra* note 54, at 35 (quoting Letter from New York State Bar Association to Committee on Military Justice 4 (Jan. 29, 1949)).

General Eisenhower, well versed in the realities of command, was not simply spouting a cliché. His statement reflected the responsibility and burden of command that remains a viable part of the system today.

a. Total Responsibility, Authority, and Lawful Influence on the System

In civil society, there is no responsibility analogous to that of a commander. The Army doctrinal definition of the commander's role captures its encompassing nature:

> Command is vested in an individual who has *total responsibility*. The essence of command is defined by the commander's competence, intuition, judgment, initiative, and character, and his ability to inspire and gain the trust of his unit. Commanders possess authority and responsibility and are accountable while in command.[540]

Some military justice reformers pay a condescending lip service to the responsibility of the commander even as they seek to take it away. For instance, the Cox Commission recognized that "[d]uring hostilities or emergencies, it is axiomatic that commanders must enjoy full and immediate disciplinary authority over those placed under their command."[541] The Commission also affirmed that it "trusts the judgment of convening authorities as well as the officers and enlisted members who are appointed to serve on courts-martial."[542] And yet the

---

[540] DEP'T OF ARMY FIELD MANUAL 101-5, STAFF ORGANIZATION AND OPERATIONS 1-1. (31 May 1997) [hereinafter FM 101-5] (emphasis added).

[541] COX COMMISSION, *supra* note 23, at 5.

[542] *Id.* at 7.

133

Commission recommended removing the commander, whom it trusts implicitly, from the military justice system.

There is a paradox at work here, the assumption that one can remove the commander from the system while still retaining its efficacy, vitality, and utility to him. This naïve aspiration clashes hard against the experiences of leaders such as General Eisenhower and General William Westmoreland, who have commanded large forces in combat and administered military justice systems. A major part of the military mission, what sets it apart from civilian life, is the "commitment to mission accomplishment in obedience to lawful authority."[543] The commander is, necessarily, the center of this world.

One might ask what any of this has to do with justice and the appointment of court members. The answer is not especially subtle, but no less true for that: Responsibility and authority must go hand in hand. Civil society recognizes the responsibility of commanders and holds them accountable even for the criminal actions of their subordinates.[544] Careers, lives, and international relations between nations can all be affected by the discipline or indiscipline of individual service members.[545] To hold a commander responsible for good

---

[543] General William C. Westmoreland and Major General George S. Prugh, *Judges in Command: The Judicialized Uniform Code of Military Justice in Combat*, 3 HARV. J.L. & PUB. POL. 2, 44 (1980).

[544] *See, e.g.*, James R. Carroll, *General's Promotion Opposed Over Handling of Gay Soldier's Death at Fort Campbell*, COURIER JOURNAL (Louisville, Kentucky), Oct. 25, 2002, at 1A, LEXIS, Newsgroup File, All (discussing efforts to block Major General Robert T. Clark's nomination to Lieutenant General based on the murder of Barry Winchell at Fort Campbell during his command); Calvin Sims, *General Bows to Show Remorse for Marine Held in Sex Offense*, THE PLAIN DEALER, Jul. 27, 2000, at 5A, LEXIS, Newsgroup File, All (recounting how the commanding general of Marine forces personally apologized to the Governor of Okinawa for an incident in which one of his 19-year-old Marines fondled a 14-year-old Okinawan girl).

[545] *See* Pamela Hess, *Army Extends Review of Kosovo Unit*, UNITED PRESS INTERNATIONAL, Oct. 4, 2000, LEXIS Newsgroup File, All (reporting that senior Army officials had ordered a review of a command climate

order and discipline without a corresponding grant of authority over the system or the

disposition of his personnel involved in it places him in an untenable position.[546] It places

the system in an untenable position.

Through his role in sending cases to courts-martial and selecting panel members, the

commander is able to exert lawful control over the military justice system.[547] The cases he

refers to courts-martial communicate his sense of acceptable and unacceptable conduct. In

appointing subordinates to courts-martial, he fulfills several goals. He reinforces his

priorities through the personnel he appoints to the court. If the courts-martial process is

meaningful to him, he appoints his most trusted subordinates, using criteria similar to what

he would employ in matching personnel with other missions; if the process means little to

him, he sends the lazy and the expendable to judge his soldiers. Either way, he sends a

message. In addition, he fulfills a training function through the operation of the military

---

that allegedly tolerated misbehavior by soldiers in 3d Battalion, 504th Parachute Infantry Regiment of the 82d Airborne Division, following the rape and murder of an 11-year-old Kosavar girl by a non-commissioned officer in the unit); Chalmers Johnson, *U.S. Armed Forces are on Tenterhooks in Okinawa; Military Island Residents Were Shocked by a Girl's Rape in 1995. What Would They Do if There was a Serious Air Accident?*, LOS ANGELES TIMES, Sep. 3, 1999, at B7, LEXIS Newsgroup File, All (discussing the repercussions when several Marines gang-raped an Okinawan girl and noting that the U.S. Marine 3d Division was almost forced to leave).

[546] *See, e.g.*, Written Comments of Walter Donovan, BrigGen USMC (ret.) to the Cox Commission, Feb. 28, 2001, *reprinted in* COX COMMISSION, *supra* note 23, app. C. General Donovan warned, with respect to removing commanders from the selection process, "Don't hobble them to administrative poohbahs, choosing their members for courts, officials who have zero operational responsibility." General Donovan recounted some of his own experiences as a commanding officer of a line unit in which he faced "daily headaches on the issue of who was available to perform 'unexpected' tasks." *Id.*

[547] *Cf.* Memorandum from John M. Economidy to Cox Commission, Subject: Appointment of Court-Martial Members by Convening Authority 1 (Nov. 28, 2000), *reprinted in* COX COMMISSION, *supra* note 23, app C. In answer to the Cox Commission's question, should court-martial members be appointed by a jury office rather than the convening authority, Mr. Economidy replied, "Absolutely not. The military mission is to fight and win wars. Maintaining discipline through the military justice system is a responsibility of the convening authority in conducting the overall military mission." *Id.*

justice system, ensuring that the next generation of leaders is prepared to administer the system.

It is important to emphasize the difference between lawful influence over the military justice system, which involves carefully selecting the cases that go to trial and the members that sit in judgment of them, and unlawful command influence, which consists of attempting to exercise coercion or unauthorized influence over the action of a court-martial or its members as to findings and sentence.[548] Lawful influence is a function of command, closely related to the core responsibilities of a commander to care for and discipline his troops. Unlawful influence is not only a crime, it is a poor management and command practice. The best commanders will avoid arbitrary and reckless meddling with the military justice system, as they would in any other aspect of command.[549] Service members are, after all, their human capital.[550]

---

[548] *See* UCMJ art. 37(a) (2002).

[549] Justice Harry Blackmun wrote of the relationship between the statutory protections of the UCMJ and the incentive a commander has to avoid arbitrary treatment of his troops:

> [T]he fearful specter of arbitrary enforcement of the articles, the engine of the dissent, is disabled, in my view, by the elaborate system of military justice that Congress has provided to servicemen, and by the self-evident, and self-selective, factor that commanders who are arbitrary with their charges will not produce the efficient and effective military organization this country needs and demands for its defense.

Parker v. Levy, 417 U.S. 733, 763-64 (1974) (Blackmun, J., concurring).

[550] *Cf.* Pound, *supra* note 21, at 24 (quoting the chief Navy spokesman to the effect that no one relishes prosecuting service personnel because they are human capital).

b. Combat and the Military Justice System

The ultimate test of the military justice system is combat, of which there are two critical aspects: its role in controlling the behavior of soldiers actually involved in combat, and its ability to operate effectively as a system under combat conditions. An effective system of military law can provide an additional motivating factor to prevent combat misconduct, which could include desertion, mistreatment of civilians, or crimes against humanity. The reality is that "[s]ervice members are frequently thrust into dirty and dangerous places, equipped with weapons of truly awesome destructive power," where they have responsibility for their own lives and the well being of many others.[551] According to Generals Westmoreland and Prugh,

> The costs of misconduct in combat are truly incalculable. . . . Because of its effect on the others, because the military law may give just the additional strength at just the right moment to prevent disastrous disobedience or flight, because it distills a *habit* of obedience to lawful orders so that compliance is second nature, for all of these reasons military law does remain as a valuable military motivator.[552]

It is axiomatic that the commander, whose authority in combat must be unquestioned, should occupy a place at the apex of the military justice system.

Operating a military justice system under combat conditions requires flexibility, ingenuity, and the ability to control resources, particularly human capital. A World War II

---

[551] Westmoreland and Prugh, *supra* note 543, at 45 (1980).

[552] *Id.* at 48.

case, *Wade v. Hunter*,[553] illustrates that combat operations can have an impact on the administration of military justice. The accused in *Wade* had been tried by a general court-martial for the rape of a German woman.[554] After the court had closed for deliberations, but before it announced findings, it requested a continuance to hear from critical witnesses who had not been able to attend the trial because of sickness.[555] Before the court could reconvene, the accused's parent unit, 76th Infantry Division, had advanced deep into Germany, far enough from the site of the offense to make it impracticable for the court-martial to reconvene. The commanding general of 76th Infantry Division withdrew the charges and transferred them to Third Army, which in turn transferred them to Fifteenth Army, the unit that now had responsibility for the town in which the offense occurred. The Fifteenth Army

---

[553] 336 U.S. 684 (1949).

[554] The facts in *Wade* illustrate how the military justice system must cope with the fast-paced environment of combat. On March 13, 1945, the 76th Infantry Division entered Krov, Germany. The next afternoon, two German women were raped by men in American uniforms. Two soldiers from the division, including the petitioner, were arrested upon charges they had committed the offense. 76th Infantry Division continued its advance. Two weeks later, it had advanced twenty-two miles into Germany to a town called Pfalzfeld, where the trial was held. The court-martial heard evidence and argument of counsel and closed to consider the case. However, later that day the court re-opened and requested a continuance to hear from the parents of the victim and also the victim's sister-in-law, who was in the room when the rape occurred and could assist in identification of the assailants. *Id.* at 685-86. 76th Infantry Division continued its advance. A week later, before the court had reconvened, the Commanding General withdrew the charges and ordered the court-martial to take no further action. He transferred the charges to his higher command, Third Army, explaining that the tactical situation had made it impossible for the division to try the case in the vicinity of the offense within a reasonable time. Third Army, meanwhile, had also advanced deeply enough into Germany that it was impracticable for any Third Army unit to try the case in the vicinity of the offense. Accordingly, the Third Army commander transferred the case to the Fifteenth Army commander, now responsible for the area in which the offense had occurred, who convened a court-martial. *Id.* at 687.

[555] This was a permissible proceeding under the Articles of War and Manual for Courts-Martial of the day. *See id.* at 691 n.7.

commander convened a new general court-martial, which convicted the accused of the rape and sentenced him to life in prison.[556]

On collateral attack, the accused sought a writ of habeas corpus, claiming he had been subjected to double jeopardy. The district court granted the writ, but the Court of Appeals reversed, and the Supreme Court affirmed. The Court recognized that the tactical situation, coupled with US Army policy that offenses would be tried in the vicinity where they occurred to facilitate the involvement of witnesses, made the unusual procedure necessary.[557]

A key factor in the Court's opinion was the recognition that the general court-martial convening authority required control over his personnel in order to carry out his tactical mission. If this meant dissolving the court-martial and transferring it to another command, so be it. "Momentous issues," wrote the Court, "hung on the invasion and we cannot assume that these court-martial officers were not needed to perform their military functions."[558] The order to dissolve the original court-martial was made by a commanding general who was "responsible for convening the court-martial and who was also responsible for the most effective military deployment of that Division in carrying out the plan for the invasion of

---

[556] At trial, the petitioner claimed double jeopardy because of the previous trial, but his motion was denied. It is unclear from the Supreme Court opinion whether the new court heard the evidence anew or relied on the record of trial. However, the court acquitted the co-accused and convicted the petitioner, sentencing him to life in prison. *Id.* at 687. An Army board of review in Europe filed a unanimous opinion that the double jeopardy claim should have been sustained. The Assistant Judge Advocate General disagreed and filed a dissenting opinion. The Commanding General of the European Theater confirmed the sentence. The petitioner filed a writ of habeas corpus with a federal district court. The circuit court of appeals reversed, and the Supreme Court affirmed. *Id.* at 692-93 (Murphy, J., dissenting).

[557] The Court relied on a long-standing rule that a trial could be discontinued "when particular circumstances manifest a necessity for so doing, and when failure to discontinue would defeat the ends of justice." *Id.* at 690.

[558] *Id.* at 692.

Germany."[559] The commander's responsibility to prosecute the war trumped his responsibility to prosecute the accused.

One should not assume that the days of courts-martial in a combat zone are over. Despite some doubt as to the vitality of the judicialized UCMJ under "military stress,"[560] Operations Desert Shield and Desert Storm demonstrated that the system could still work under combat conditions. First Armored Division conducted three general courts-martial, one special court-martial, and six summary courts during the four months that the division participated in Desert Shield and Desert Storm.[561] Two of the general courts-martial and the special court-martial were held within days of the beginning of combat operations.[562] Conducting the courts-martial required the dedication of resources available only to the command: a UH-60 Black Hawk helicopter to ferry the trial counsel, defense counsel, and military judge to field locations, generators, tents, and personnel.[563] A third general court-martial, fully contested, featured court proceedings held in three countries: Saudi Arabia, Iraq, and Kuwait.[564]

The 1st Armored Division commander was able to use the military justice system to reinforce discipline at a critical time. Soldiers in the division were "surprised, if not

---

[559] *Id.* at 691-92.

[560] *See, e.g.*, Westmoreland & Prugh, *supra* note 543, at 4 (based on over-judicialization of the UCMJ, authors conclude that it is incapable of performing its intended role during time of military stress).

[561] FREDERIC L. BORCH, JUDGE ADVOCATES IN COMBAT: ARMY LAWYERS IN MILITARY OPERATIONS FROM VIETNAM TO HAITI 188 (2001).

[562] *Id.*

[563] *See id.* at 188-90.

[564] *Id.* at 189.

shocked" upon learning that a court-martial would be held the night before the attack on Iraq was to begin, but it sent a lawful message to them that high standards were important to their commander.[565]

A commander who has no control over the disposition of court-martial personnel will have little incentive to use the military justice system in a combat zone. In the Desert Storm example, a court-martial selection method that used random procedures or the edicts of a far-off "administrative poohbah" or central court-martial administrator would have interfered considerably with the commander's judgment to employ the personnel under his command as he saw fit. With random selection, the commander could not have predicted which officers would be required for a court-martial panel. Because of the potential impact on operations, he might have resisted the decision or put off the court-martial until a later date, thereby losing the advantages of holding the proceedings in a combat zone on the eve of combat. He also might have resisted the idea of providing tents, generators, and helicopters to a central court-martial administrator from a far-off command. Conversely, a central court-martial administrator might not have shared the commander's view of the seriousness of the offense or the necessity of trying it on location just prior to the commencement of operations.

In short, the military justice system must retain its martial roots and character in order to fulfill its varied missions. The commander must always have the flexibility and control over personnel or resources in order to ensure that the military justice system meets the needs of

---

[565] *Id.* at 190.

his command under a variety of circumstances. The current system offers such flexibility; the reforms, despite their assurances to the contrary, do not.

2. How the Current System Benefits the Accused

The JSC has recognized that "public perceptions of the court-martial member selection process are often based on limited information and misunderstanding."[566] Worse, legal commentators tend to feed on this, generally focusing their criticisms on misperceptions.[567] In turn, these criticisms have spilled over to the popular press. A recent article in a national news magazine picks up the claim that the system is unfair because the convening authority wields prosecutorial discretion, hand-picks the jury, has the ability to approve findings and sentence, and exercises clemency power.[568] The article cites the military's courts-martial conviction rate as proof that the system is actually unfair and is stacked to convict.[569] A public that bases its opinions of the military justice system on published misperceptions and misleading comparisons with the civilian criminal justice system cannot be expected to have either an accurate or favorable view of the military justice system.

If we change the frame of reference, perhaps the system will not seem so one-sided and unfair. When evaluated in terms of the benefits it offers to the accused--particularly in

---

[566] JSC REPORT, *supra* note 29, at 47.

[567] *Id.*

[568] *See* Pound, *supra* note 21, at 21-22.

[569] *Id.* at 22 (claiming a 97% conviction rate for courts-martial in FY 2001). Of course, the article does not bother to compare the military conviction rate with civilian conviction rates, fails to differentiate between convictions and guilty pleas, and neglects to break down the conviction rate by type of court-martial.

comparison to the civilian jury system--discretionary convening authority selection of panel members appears to be a fair system that confers significant due process and tactical advantages to an accused.

So, let us posit the average, reasonable citizen, someone who knows little about the military justice system but has an open mind and is willing to learn. It stands to reason that such a person would benefit from an accurate introduction to the courts-martial panel process, from selection and appointment through trial.

a. Selection Process and Panel-Member Qualifications

Suppose that this citizen were to learn how the actual assignment process took place. Would she find it shocking that a commander, using information provided to him by subordinate staff specialists and subordinate commanders, selects members on a best-qualified basis using criteria of age, education, experience, training, length of service, and judicial temperament?[570] Would it make a difference to the citizen if she understood that the commander has total responsibility for all operational aspects of command, including the disposition and assignment of personnel?[571] How would she feel if she knew the accused would face a panel of individuals with considerable experience with military society and a

---

[570] UCMJ art. 25(d)(2) (2002). *See also* Lamb, *supra* note 22, at 128-29 (discussing the common method for member selection by which a convening authority solicits nominations from subordinate commanders for his consideration based on the criteria of UCMJ art. 25(d)(2) and noting that historically, more than 87% of jurisdictions use this method). *See also* Young, *supra* note 22, at 104-105 (noting that most general court-martial convening authorities must rely on subordinates and special staff officers for nominations).

[571] *See* FM 101-5, *supra* note 540, at 1-1.

higher education level than the typical civilian jury?[572] What if she learned that a court-martial panel, unlike a civilian jury, is also charged with the judicial function to pass sentence on the accused?[573] The citizen might be favorably impressed with a system that produces "blue-ribbon panels," particularly if she were aware that the civilian jury system has come under attack because random selection methods tend to produce juries with lower education levels and experience, thereby degrading the quality of justice in civilian courts.[574]

b. Forum Selection Rights

Suppose this citizen knew that the military accused, unlike his civilian counterpart, had the absolute right to select the type of forum that would hear his case--judge alone, officer panel or, in the case of enlisted personnel, a panel consisting of officers and at least one-third enlisted personnel?[575] What if she learned that an accused could make his decision with prior

---

[572] As the Court of Military Appeals has observed, UCMJ Article 25(d)(2) criteria can tend to produce relatively senior panels. *See* United States v. Nixon, 33 M.J. 433, 434 (C.M.A. 1991). The military has a higher level of formal education than civilian society. Of the civilian population, 24.3% have a bachelor's degree or higher, whereas 89.9% of officers have a bachelor's degree or higher. In the enlisted ranks, more than 97.4% have at least a high school diploma/GED or higher, compared to 82.8% of the civilian population. *See* MFRC Report, *supra* note 389.

[573] *See* UCMJ art. 51(a) (2002) (discussing voting procedures by members of a court-martial on findings and sentence). *See also* MCM, *supra* note 5, R.C.M. 1006 (establishing the procedures members must use in proposing and voting for sentences).

[574] Some commentators believe that random selection methods tend to be skewed towards selection of less educated and experienced segments of society. The better-educated members of society are often able to escape jury duty, and during voir dire, lawyers tend to use peremptory challenges to strike educated jury members. *See* Douglas G. Smith, *The Historical and Constitutional Contexts of Jury Reform*, 25 HOFTSTRA L. REV. 377, 458-469 (1996). A proposed solution is to select jurors using criteria such as education or previous trial experience. *Id.* at 457.

[575] *Compare* UCMJ art. 16 (2002) (classifying the types of courts-martial and granting the accused the right to choose trial by members or by judge alone) *and id.* art. 25(c)(1) (granting an enlisted accused the right to demand trial by general or special courts-martial with a membership consisting of no less than one-third enlisted personnel) *with* FED. R. CRIM. P. 23(a) (granting a criminal defendant the right to trial by judge alone only if the judge and the prosecutor agree to it). In the Federal criminal system, the prosecutor is the gatekeeper of the

knowledge of the individuals who would be on the panel and had access to their personnel

files and the ability to inquire into their reputations for justice and fairness?[576] And that after

examining this information, could still elect trial by judge alone if he didn't like what he saw

on the panels? These procedures grant greater rights to a military accused than are available

to his civilian counterpart.

   c. The Panel at Trial

Suppose the citizen knew that an accused on trial for a serious offense would be fully

acquitted and would not have to endure a hung jury and a re-trial if just one-third of the panel

was not convinced beyond a reasonable doubt?[577] What if she were aware that through the

judicious use of challenges, the accused's counsel could actually stack the numbers

statistically in his favor for acquittal?[578] What if the citizen knew that at trial the members of

the panel would listen to the evidence, take notes, [579] question witnesses,[580] and engage

meaningfully in the process?[581]

---

accused's forum rights; there is no Constitutional right to a trial by judge alone. *See* United States v. Singer, 380 U.S. 24 (1965) (upholding the procedure of Fed. R. Crim. P. 23(a) and noting that there is no Constitutional right to trial by judge alone).

[576] *See* Young, *supra* note 22, at 117-118 (noting that in practice, but not as a matter of right, convening authorities have permitted the accused to know the names of the court members before electing a forum).

[577] UCMJ art. 52(a)(2) (2002) (two-thirds majority required for conviction). *See also* UCMJ art. 60(e)(2) (2002) (forbidding reconsideration or revision of any finding of not guilty of any specification).

[578] *See* Smallridge, *supra* note 22, at 375-379 (thoroughly explaining the "numbers game" and providing a statistical analysis of court membership that is favorable to the accused).

[579] *See* MCM, *supra* note 5, R.C.M. 921 (explaining that members can take their notes, if any, with them into deliberations).

What if the citizen understood the sanctity of oaths to the military mind and realized that integrity is a way of life to most service members?[582] And suppose the citizen knew that the UCMJ absolutely forbids any attempts to influence the action of a court-martial in any way, including performance ratings of the court members or counsel?[583] As an additional protection to the accused, members in a court-martial vote by secret written ballot,[584] in contrast to the open voting in a civilian jury.

A citizen who knew all these things but was aware of the conviction rate at military courts-martial might nevertheless question a system in which the vast majority of accused were convicted. However, could we not expect her mind to change if she knew that the

---

[580] *See* MCM, *supra* note 5, MIL. R. EVID. 614 (granting all parties, including the members, the right to call, question, cross-examine, or recall witnesses at courts-martial).

[581] Again, these are areas where military courts-martial practice is superior to civilian practice. A jury that cannot question witnesses is hindered in its ability to function as a fact finder. Civilian jurors typically are not permitted to take notes or question witnesses. Some have suggested that permitting them to do so would improve the quality of justice, because note-taking aids in recollection of the evidence, focuses the attention of the juror on the proceedings, and lessens the time for deliberation. *See* Smith, *supra* note 574, at 496-501.

[582] An excellent example of this occurred in the trial of Lieutenant William Calley for the My Lai massacre. A member of the panel, Colonel Ford, received orders to refrain from any exposure to news accounts of the My Lai massacre nearly one year before the trial was actually held. During that year, whenever he saw a news flash about My Lai on the television, he left the room, and whenever he saw a newspaper headline about My Lai, he read no further. *See* Calley vs. Callaway, 519 F.2d 184, 211 (5th Cir. 1975). This type of integrity and obedience to orders is by no means atypical in the military, and the accused benefits greatly from panel members who have taken an oath "to faithfully and impartially try, according to the evidence, their conscience, and the laws applicable to trials by court martial, the case of the accused now before this court." U.S. DEP'T OF ARMY, PAM. 27-9, MILITARY JUDGES' BENCHBOOK para. 2-5 (1 May 2002).

[583] UCMJ art. 37 forbids any person subject to the code from trying to influence the action of a court-martial in any way. Furthermore, the article forbids any person subject to the Code from considering or evaluating a court member's duty on a court-martial as part of an effectiveness, fitness, or efficiency report. *See* UCMJ art. 37 (2002).

[584] *See id.* art. 51(a) (providing for vote by secret written ballot on findings, sentence, and challenges when there is no military judge present).

conviction rate for contested courts-martial and contested jury cases was almost exactly the same?[585]

Now, suppose this citizen became aware that reformers wanted to change the military justice system to remove the commander from the process and introduce jury selection concepts such as random selection. Initially, one might expect her to view this favorably; most people accept the idea that juries are the bulwarks of freedom. But let us suppose she also learned the truth about reform efforts, that they offer only illusory change, that every single reform effort rigs the random selection system because the consequences of statistically honest random selection are inconceivable to reformers and incompatible with military needs. Moreover, reforms do double damage by increasing the administrative burden on the command and, in changing the criteria from "best qualified" to "merely available," degrading the quality of the panels. Centralizing the court administrative functions, as has been done in Great Britain, brings with it delay and inefficiency. The result is a system whose usefulness to the commander has been greatly compromised.

---

[585] In fact, the conviction rate for general courts-martial is actually slightly lower than for felonies in federal district courts or in the 75 largest metropolitan areas of the United States. The overall conviction rate for general courts-martial in fiscal year 2001 was 95% (1675 convictions out of 1756 total cases in the services combined). This figure was obtained by adding together the total reported general courts-martial convictions from the Army, Navy (including the Marines), Air Force, and Coast Guard and dividing by the total reported number of general courts-martial held). *See* CODE COMMITTEE ON MILITARY JUSTICE, ANNUAL REPORT (2001), *available at* http://www.armfor.uscourts.gov/Annual.htm. In the federal system, the conviction rate for felonies (including guilty pleas) that were not dismissed was 98.37% percent. This figure was obtained by dividing the total number of convictions in the federal system (68,156) by the total number of cases that were not dismissed (69,283). *See* SOURCEBOOK OF CRIMINAL JUSTICE STATISTICS 414 (Ann L. Pastore & Kathleen Maguire, eds.) (2001), *available at* http://www.albany.edu/sourcebook/. In the 75 largest metropolitan areas, the felony conviction rate was approximately 95%. *See id.* at 452. In the early 1970's, General Hodson discussed the fallacy of arguments that the military justice system is unfair because of its conviction rates. He noted that the rate was nearly the same for the military (94%) as for the civilian system (96%) on cases that went to trial. A high acquittal rate, he observed, can indicate that improper cases are going to juries or that prosecutors are unprepared. *See* Hodson, *supra* note 22, at 52.

One would expect that an informed citizen, aware of all the facts, would look favorably upon the rights offered by the military justice panel system to the accused. Selection of panel members is, like many other decisions a commander makes, simply another exercise of operational responsibilities. It provides a benefit to the commander because, by selecting his best-qualified subordinates, he ensures the high quality of justice meted out to his soldiers and demonstrates his commitment and vision that justice is important to him. The system is fair and flexible, and it offers the military accused choices that are unavailable to civilian criminal defendants. The panels are well educated, honest, and faithful to their oaths. The accused has a statistically similar likelihood of acquittal in a military court, but has the benefit of using the panel system and the two-thirds majority rule to structure the panel in his favor.

The system of command control of military justice meets the needs of the command and the nation, but just as important, it meets the needs of the accused. The statutory framework Congress created in the UCMJ strikes a balance that should not lightly be disturbed. At this point in history, it is fair to assume that the Framers and several generations of Congress knew what they were doing in retaining a system of command control over panel member appointment.

V. Conclusion

William Winthrop once warned against the hasty and intemperate revision of the American military justice system. He wrote,

Our military code, however, stands alone among our public statutes in its retaining many provisions and forms of expression dating back from two hundred to five hundred years . . . any radical remodeling which would divest this time-honored body of law of its historical associations and interest would be greatly to be deprecated.[586]

The practice of discretionary convening authority selection of court-martial panel members dates back centuries and has been an integral part of the American military justice system since the Revolution. It is deeply rooted in the earliest efforts of armies to employ military tribunals as a means of ensuring good order and discipline while providing due process and fundamental fairness to the accused. The United States Congress, which has the Constitutional responsibility to make rules for the government of the armed forces, has consistently rejected efforts to remove the convening authority from the process of selecting panel members. In promulgating the UCMJ in the late 1940s, Congress struck a delicate balance between individual rights and the power of commanders to administer the military justice system.

Modern-day reformers seek to upset that balance. The UCMJ has proven its worth as a fair system of justice that grants due process to individuals while preserving the flexibility, efficiency, and ease of administration that are necessary in a military setting. No one seriously questions its actual fairness. Nevertheless, concerned that the role of the convening authority in selecting panel members presents the appearance of evil, many seek to remove the convening authority from the panel selection process, replacing him with either a central courts-martial administrator or with modified versions of the random selection system used

---

[586] WINTHROP, *supra* note 3, at 24.

in the Federal courts. In *United States v. Wiesen*, a judicially activist majority of the CAAF has demonstrated a willingness to place significant limits on the ability of commanders to select subordinate commanders to serve on courts-martial panels. Because of *Wiesen*, commanders are no longer free to choose their best-qualified subordinates to serve on panels if a certain percentage of them are from the same chain of command.

It is time to fight back in defense of a system that produces "better educated and more conscientious panels . . . than any other system would."[587] To counter the damage done by *Wiesen*, the President should use his rule-making authority under UCMJ Article 36(a) to amend the Manual for Courts-Martial and make clear his intent that command and supervisory arrangements are no impediment to service on courts-martial panels. In the long term, proponents of the system must shift the terms of the debate. So long as reformers can fight on ground of their own choosing, they will have the upper hand. Conversely, when the question of panel member selection is cast in terms of its proper Constitutional context, its utility to commanders, its fairness to the soldier, and its relationship to the purposes of military justice, it becomes evident that Congress struck the proper balance in retaining the convening authority's discretionary ability to select panel members.

Honor, integrity, and trustworthiness define the character of American military commanders, just as discipline and adherence to the rule of law form the backbone of the most effective military the world has ever known. Congress has always retained the commander as the central figure in the military justice system, no doubt recognizing that

---

[587] Cooke, *supra* note 22.

"[t]here is a fundamental anomaly that vests a commander with life-or-death authority over his troops in combat but does not trust that same commander to make a sound decision with respect to justice and fairness to the individual."[588] Divesting convening authorities of the power to appoint panel members in order to attain a more idealistically pure system of justice elevates form over substance and proclaims that the military justice system is more important than the military. Such a result, to borrow a phrase from Winthrop, "would be greatly to be deprecated."

---

[588] Westmoreland and Prugh, *supra* note 543, at 58 (1980).

Appendix A: Proposed Rule Changes

Note: new language is underlined.

R.C.M. 503(a)(4):

(4) *Members with a command or supervisory relationship.* The Convening Authority may detail members with a command or supervisory relationship with other members and such relationships are not disqualifying.

Analysis

This section is intended to clarify that the rules of procedure in trial by courts-martial do not disqualify members with command or supervisory relationships from serving on courts-martial. Specific grounds for challenge of members and related procedures are in RCM 912(f). The existence of command or supervisory relationships among members, including a number sufficient to convict, does not constitute grounds for challenge under RCM 912(f)(1)(N). *See* United States v. Greene, 43 C.M.R. 72, 78 (1970) ("Congress, in its wisdom, made all commissioned officers eligible for consideration to serve on courts-martial [subject to the limitations contained in Article 25, UCMJ]."). In 1968, Congress amended Article 37, UCMJ, by adding subparagraph (b), prohibiting anyone preparing an effectiveness, fitness, or efficiency report (or any other such document) from "(1) consider[ing] or evaluat[ing] the performance of duty of any such member as a member of a court-martial." UCMJ art. 37(b) (2002). *See also* RCM 912(f), Analysis.

R.C.M. 912(f)(1)(N):

(N) Should not sit as a member in the interest of having the court-martial free from substantial doubt as to legality, fairness, and impartiality. The existence of a command or supervisory relationship between two or more members of a court-martial panel (even where such members constitute a majority sufficient to reach a finding of guilty) shall not constitute grounds for removal for cause.

Discussion

Examples of matters which may be grounds for challenge under subsection (N) are that the member: has a direct personal interest in the result of the trial; is closely related to the accused, a counsel, or a witness in the case; has participated as a member or counsel in the trial of a closely related case; has a decidedly friendly or hostile attitude toward a party; or has an inelastic opinion concerning an appropriate sentence for the offenses charged.

The second sentence of subsection (N) is intended to clarify that factors to be considered under Rule 912(f) do not include the existence of command or supervisory relationships among the members of a court-martial panel. The existence of such relationships do not evidence "implied bias" or otherwise constitute a violation of this Rule. As such, the second sentence is intended to overrule the holding of the Court of Appeals for the Armed Forces in *United States v. Wiesen*, 56 M.J. 172 (2001).

Analysis

In light of the finding in *United States v. Wiesen*, 56 M.J. 172 (2001), *pet. for recons. denied*, 57 MJ 48 (2002), this section is intended to clarify the President's position that command or supervisory relationships between members, even where such members constitute a majority sufficient for conviction, are not a basis for removals for cause. It is common for courts-martial members to have command or supervisory relationships with other members. Such relationships between two or more members of a court-martial panel (even where such members constitute a number sufficient to reach a finding of guilty) are not grounds for challenge under this rule. *See, e.g.*, United States v. Blocker, 32 M.J. 281, 286-287 (CMA 1991) (noting that the mere fact of a rating or senior-subordinate relationship between members does not generally give rise to a challenge for cause and observing that "the omnipresence of these relationships suggests a sua sponte inquiry by judge was not required"); United States v. Murphy, 26 M.J. 454, 455 (CMA 1988) ("We hold that the Court of Military Review erred as a matter of law in applying a per se disqualification predicated solely on the fact that a senior member of the court-martial is involved in writing or endorsing the effectiveness reports of junior members."); United States v. Bannwarth, 36 M.J. 265, 268 (CMA 1984) (finding that "a senior-subordinate relationship between court members does not automatically disqualify the senior member"); United States v. Deain, 5 U.S.C.M.A. 44, 17 C.M.R. 44, 52 (1954) ("It may be conceded that the mere fact that the senior, or other member of the court, coincidentally has the duty to prepare and submit a fitness report on a junior member, in and of itself, does not affect the junior's 'sense of responsibility and individual integrity by which men judge men.'") (citations omitted).